THE
TRANSFORMATION
FACTOR

LEADING YOUR COMPANY
FOR **GOOD,** FOR **GOD,**
AND FOR **GROWTH**

THE
TRANSFORMATION
FACTOR

J. FRANK HARRISON III

GREENLEAF
BOOK GROUP PRESS

Scripture taken from the New King James Version®. Copyright © 1982 by Thomas Nelson. Used by permission. All rights reserved.

Scripture quotations marked (NIV) are taken from the Holy Bible, New International Version®, NIV®. Copyright © 1973, 1978, 1984, 2011 by Biblica, Inc.™ Used by permission of Zondervan. All rights reserved worldwide. www.zondervan.com The "NIV" and "New International Version" are trademarks registered in the United States Patent and Trademark Office by Biblica, Inc.™

Grateful acknowledgment is made to the following for permission to reproduce Dr. Martin Luther King Jr.'s Speech to Barratt Junior High School Students in Philadelphia in 1967.

Reprinted by arrangement with The Heirs to the Estate of Martin Luther King Jr., c/o Writers House as agent for the proprietor New York, NY. Copyright © 1967 by Dr. Martin Luther King, Jr. Renewed © 1995 by Coretta Scott King.

Published by Greenleaf Book Group Press
Austin, Texas
www.gbgpress.com

Distributed by Greenleaf Book Group

For ordering information or special discounts for bulk purchases, please contact Greenleaf Book Group at PO Box 91869, Austin, TX 78709, 512.891.6100.

Design and composition by Greenleaf Book Group
Cover design by Greenleaf Book Group
Cover Images: ©iStockphoto/ihoe and ©iStockphoto/Michael Burrell

Publisher's Cataloging-in-Publication data is available.

Print ISBN: 978-1-62634-844-8

eBook ISBN: 978-1-62634-845-5

Part of the Tree Neutral® program, which offsets the number of trees consumed in the production and printing of this book by taking proactive steps, such as planting trees in direct proportion to the number of trees used: www.treeneutral.com

TreeNeutral®

Printed in the United States of America on acid-free paper

21 22 23 24 25 26   10 9 8 7 6 5 4 3 2 1

First Edition

This book is dedicated to my dear friend Bob Pettus who passed away in 2017. Bob served me so well as mentor, coach, advisor, counselor, and friend.

Bob came to our company in 1984 as VP of human resources. He was a man of great integrity, character, and capabilities. He was trustworthy, a connector, a negotiator, a teacher, and the list goes on.

He was respected and, therefore, followed by our leaders. He was the one to stand up and lead our company transformation from a normal, political, messy business culture to a purpose-driven culture that honors God, serves others, pursues excellence, and grows profitably.

Bob came to Coke Consolidated with a God-given purpose. He fulfilled his calling and has left a powerful legacy. Thank you, Bob, for the eternal impact you are having on our people.

CONTENTS

I believe that one of the next great moves of God is going to be through the believers in the workplace.[1]

—Billy Graham

FOREWORD

I am a HUGE J. Frank Harrison fan for many reasons, but perhaps the most important is that he models what I have communicated in my three best-selling books, *Love Does*, *Everybody Always*, and *Dream Big*. I have had a chance to spend time with him, his wife Jan, and some of his leaders at Open Eyes nonprofit events and now know we share several things in common. Frank is gutsy and models a bold bias for action in every area of his life—he gets "love . . . does!" He is also a man of deep compassion and extraordinary generosity. His confident humility guides his daily actions as Chairman of the largest Coca-Cola bottling company in the United States. He and his sixteen thousand plus team members are rapidly becoming one of the most highly regarded companies in the world.

As an author, I know how important it is to "smoke what I am selling" and model what I write about in my books. To do otherwise would be hypocritical! I also know it can be incredibly challenging to take the things I think and write about as an author and actually make them happen. Fortunately, for Frank, he has been "making things happen" since assuming his role as Chairman at Coke Consolidated nearly three decades ago and has now written an authentic and transparent account of his transformational leadership journey for our benefit. You might say, he did it first and only now is getting around to writing about it. Ever since our first meeting, I have been fascinated by the many ways he acts on his personal faith and convictions to shape not only his company but also the global marketplace.

I enjoyed reading *The Transformation Factor* because it was like sitting down with Frank for an intimate conversation and letting his stories "shake up my snow globe" as he challenged and supported me to become a culture-shaping leader. The stories Frank tells are personal, professional, and deeply compelling.

Frank is a reflective practitioner who thinks deeply about what he does with what has been entrusted to him. In fact, he will tell you one day he will be held accountable for what he has done with all of it. Many years ago, that epiphany became a defining moment for him, a wake-up call to stop thinking and start acting. And act, he has. In my first book *Love Does*, I wrote, "I used to be afraid at failing at what matters, now I am afraid of succeeding at things that don't matter." Throughout the book you have in your hands, Frank will guide you, the reader, chapter by chapter into a conversation about the things that really matter. I was especially challenged by the "work it out" and "one-on-one" exercises at the end of each chapter that can be used for both personal and group reflection. It felt like I had a coach by my side as I wrestled with each thought, question, or exercise.

The millions of people who have responded to my own books leads me to believe *The Transformation Factor* will be a smashing success. I can confidently assert this because Frank Harrison is the type of transformational leader and Christ follower highlighted in all of my work.

Together, as we all work to create a culture where others can compose lives of meaning and service, let's continue to learn from one another. To begin or continue your journey to be a transformational leader, read on and plan to attend a regularly scheduled upcoming t-factor global conference, which you can learn more about in the back of the book.

To share this book with you is a special honor, and I know Frank and I look forward to hearing the stories of personal and corporate transformation from you so that together, we can continue to grow as culture shapers.

—Bob Goff

Bob Goff is a lawyer, a speaker, and the author of the *New York Times* best-selling books *Love Does* and *Everybody, Always*. Goff currently works with Love Does, formerly known as Restore International, a non-profit organization he founded.

AUTHOR'S NOTE

It means the world to me that you'd take time out of your busy schedule to read this book. So, first things first—thank you! As you read, you might be tempted to think of me and the company I work for as being The Coca-Cola Company, but that's not the case. Many people don't know that The Coca-Cola Company, which makes its company headquarters in Atlanta, Georgia, owns the Coca-Cola brand and produces the concentrate that makes that Coke in your hand so refreshing.

Though I have a great relationship with many fine folks at The Coca-Cola Company, our company is an independent Coca-Cola bottler. I serve as chairman and CEO of Coca-Cola Consolidated, the largest Coca-Cola bottler in the United States. In total, we make, sell, and distribute more than three hundred brands and flavors across fourteen states and the District of Columbia, in the Southeast, Midwest, and Mid-Atlantic portion of the United States. We currently

have twelve manufacturing facilities and seventy-seven distribution and sales centers employing over sixteen thousand
people. Our corporate offices are located in Charlotte, North
Carolina; we are a publicly traded company on the NASDAQ
under the symbol COKE.

I'll touch on the very interesting history between The Coca-
Cola Company and Coca-Cola Consolidated later on in the
book. I just wanted you to begin this reading journey with
the understanding of the difference between the companies.
Thanks again; I hope you enjoy the book.

All my best,
J. Frank Harrison III
Chairman and CEO,
Coca-Cola Consolidated

....

FORGING NEW PATHS

I n 1886, John Pemberton, a pharmacist in Atlanta, Georgia, began experimenting with potions and concoctions in the backroom of his little shop. In those days, a pharmacist might well mix up a cough syrup to treat some illness using common herbs. But near the turn of the twentieth century, with the Industrial Revolution being felt in every sector and field of business, pharmacies carried drugs made en masse. Capsules and pills were sold to the public. And in the 1890s, aspirin was invented and sold by Bayer. I read an article once that suggested the main ingredient in aspirin, salicylic acid, is found in herbs like jasmine, clover, and trees. It was a time when pharmacists still mixed up remedies for folks, but there was growing competition with the big drug companies, which had begun doing the mixing and then asking the pharmacists to sell the pharmaceuticals. I'm thankful that Mr. Pemberton still experimented; otherwise, the world would be without one of its favorite beverages.

It was the day and age of the traveling salesman hawking the latest and greatest elixir. You get the picture.

I'm not sure what drove John Pemberton in his experiments. I'm sure it took experimenting with a few batches before he came up with something really special: *the secret formula.*

That formula for the syrup became the primary ingredient for the global mega-brand Coca-Cola. It was Pemberton's partner and bookkeeper, Frank M. Robinson, who named the syrup Coca-Cola.[2] Even today, the secret formula remains guarded like Fort Knox—protected, hidden away, yet used every day to make the best-selling soft drink worldwide. They say the daily servings of Coca-Cola beverages are near 1.9 billion globally.

But the sale of Coca-Cola products is just one aspect of the secret formula. Coca-Cola is one of the most recognized brands in the world. Currently, a quick Google search on the most recognized word in the world reveals "Coca-Cola" is the second-most recognizable word in the world behind the word "OK."

The incredible brand legacy of Coca-Cola began by creating the right formula. Though I'm thankful for this particular secret formula, not all worthwhile or meaningful things in life come from a secret formula.

NO SECRET TO THE FORMULA

It'd be nice if we could concoct a secret formula to deal with the hardships we face in life each day. But just when you think you have life figured out, it throws you a curve ball, and just like that, you're back at square one.

We learn quickly in life that there's no back-alley formula-making shop for true life change. When things get hard, you can't fix them with a magic concoction. If life has taught me anything it's that if you need to hit the reset button, there's no secret to the formula for personal and vocational transformation. Just hard work, tough decisions, and a never-give-up mindset. And oh yeah, faith—the most important element, in my opinion. These things might sound like ingredients for a formula, but in reality, you can't throw these into a pot and *poof*, everything's fixed. Instead, I like to think of these things as building blocks for change.

And like all building blocks, they need a skilled craftsman to create something remarkable, something that will last, something that will change lives. At some level, *I believe we're all leaders.* Maybe you are not leading in a large company. Maybe you're a small business owner. Or perhaps you're a professor or even a homeschool mom or dad? Those contexts require leadership. Are you a mother or father? Leadership required. Oh, you're single and living in an apartment just going to work every day. Guess what, you're still a leader. You must lead yourself, make good decisions, and act responsibly.

You see, these building blocks apply to us all.

A NEW TYPE OF LEADER

Lasting change in a person's life or in the life of their business requires a new breed of leader, someone who can approach a difficult situation with grit, confidence, perseverance, and faith.

"But wait, Frank, that sounds like every other leader-type person."

I agree. This particular type of leader, however, also looks beyond the typical growth metrics of a company and into its heart and soul. What makes it tick? What will set it apart? What greater purpose does it serve?

In the corporate world, we live in a culture where businesses and their leaders live under the microscope. Leaders must consider not only their bottom line but also the health of their company—and that's a good thing! The health of a company is not only measured in outputs and return on investments. It is, more importantly, measured by the corporate culture and by the hearts of the individuals who support the company through their physical and intellectual effort. Every person in an organization matters, and how they are led matters just as much.

And what about on the personal side? Leading our families, ourselves, our churches, and our communities requires people to care for one another, to value generosity, and to be honest. I'm certainly far from being a leadership guru, but I have learned lessons in life that have convinced me of the need to change not only my approach to corporate leadership but also my approach to leading in other areas of my personal life. This book is my attempt to articulate those lessons.

The world loves to tell you how to live, what to buy, and even who to be. We see celebrity business people and aspire to be like those men and women on television or featured in *The Wall Street Journal.* And under the pressure to be like these people and mimic their success, we can easily lose ourselves and get sidetracked from our purpose in work and life.

But you and I don't have to live and work according to the rules of the world. We can forge new paths in business and in our personal lives, paths marked with the deep values that make life meaningful and give purpose to our vocations.

If you want to learn how to transform your work environment into a place of vitality, growth, and health, by all means, keep reading. And if you're looking for some nuggets on how to apply those same lessons to your personal life, then this book just might be up your alley.

....

CHAPTER 1

THE TRANSFORMATIONAL LEADER

*I alone cannot change the world, but I can cast a
stone across the waters to create many ripples.*

—Mother Teresa

*Transformation is a process, and as life happens there are tons of
ups and downs. It's a journey of discovery—there are moments
on mountaintops and moments in deep valleys of despair.*

—Rick Warren

When this life is all said and done, how will people remember you? Have you ever thought about that? When your kids have all grown, and you move past the big five-oh, you begin to look at life differently, and you consider what the idea of legacy really means.

A few years ago, I read a book by a highly successful businessman who founded a company in his garage back in the 1970s. The company grew to be a $5 billion company and continues to grow. He told the story of his upbringing and how his family didn't have a lot of material possessions. He explained how his faith was shaped by his parents' faith and what he learned by the principles they instilled in him.

The rest of the book dealt with what he learned about legacy and his plan to give away the bulk of his monetary empire to charity. Of course, when someone says they're going to give away all their money, people tend to perk up and take notice. I sure did.

He explained how legacy was more than leaving behind a company or mountains of cash for your children and grandchildren. He had no desire to leave something that, in the hands of the young and immature, can corrupt and lead even the best people astray. He emphasized that legacy begins with who you are and who you are becoming. In short, a legacy is more than money and things.

Of course, I'd heard similar perspectives on legacy before, as I'm sure you have too. But this time, the idea of legacy stuck with me. I thought back over my own story and upbringing. I also reflected on my early days at our company and how I was leading as chairman and CEO. Was I building a legacy that was more than achievements and money and things?

A series of memories flooded my mind. I remembered the early lessons I learned: lessons of what not to do as a business leader, lessons about loyalty and dedication, lessons about trust. But I also thought about the incredible change our company has experienced over the past two decades. Our company has transformed from what I believe a typical corporate culture looks like into a life-giving environment that draws top talent in our industry. People *want* to work for us, and trust me, that wasn't always the case.

I realized that if I wrote a book, I could tell readers these stories of transformation and illustrate what a transformational leader looks like. I'd tell them about the heartbeat of the transformational leader, which is service. That's right, the transformational leader is a servant leader. And I'd tell them the incredible impact this brand of leadership had on our employees and our community.

The book in your hands is precisely that.

Imagine if you and I enjoyed a glass of refreshing Coca-Cola as I told you the stories and lessons about leadership and transformation that I've learned over the past forty years. We'd probably drink a lot of Coca-Cola, because I can talk about this stuff for days. I'm a storyteller by nature. If you ask me something about leadership, I'll answer with a story. And if you and I were chatting with our Cokes, I'd probably begin with a story about a twenty-two-year-old man who didn't wait until later in life to plant the seeds of his legacy. I would tell you about my only son, James.

THE SEEDS OF LEGACY AND THE ACTS OF TRANSFORMATION

In 2005, when James was twenty-two years old, a friend at Samaritan's Purse challenged him to get involved in bringing relief and aid to the war-torn area of Sudan. If you don't already know, Samaritan's Purse is a global Christian humanitarian aid organization that provides assistance for people in spiritual and physical need.

James was a go-getter, so I wasn't too surprised when he jumped at the opportunity to make a difference and throw himself into a place filled with danger. Not only did James possess a passion for living life, but he also loved adventure and relished risk. Most of all, he enjoyed helping people. James accepted the challenge from our friends at Samaritan's Purse and left for Lui, Sudan, which at that time was still embroiled in its civil war with the north.

The invitation proved to be a wake-up call for James. During his time in Sudan, he visited burned villages. He met with lone survivors from brutal attacks that destroyed whole communities, and he visited hurting people in hospitals and clinics. He traveled into hard-to-reach villages with pastors and evangelists. He discovered just how ravaged this area of the world was with war and disease. It broke his heart. But it also ignited it. The experience gripped James and inspired him to make a difference. He decided to be an agent of change.

James was eager to spread the word about the deep need he discovered. I remember how he'd call me and my wife, Jan, from Africa and tell us stories about what he had experienced and his desire to do something about it. In fact, he turned our friends' challenge on to me.

"Dad," he said, "we have to help these people."

James didn't see a country or a town or a village in need. He saw individual people with names and families of their own in need. I loved his perspective.

He saw individuals.

He listened to their stories.

He became part of their culture.

And they loved him for it.

Our Sudanese friend Gabriel said, "I've never seen anyone else love our people like James. He became like them; he worked, lived, slept, and ate among them." Of course, being a father, this is the kind of praise from other people you dream about for your children. I was proud of James and inspired by him.

Seeing James's passion for helping these beautiful people was nothing short of remarkable; he had discovered and was living out his purpose right where God had called him. How could I not accept the challenge and work with him to make a difference in the lives of people in great need? With James as our guide, I began taking trips to remote parts of Africa with others to see the ravages of war, disease, and poverty with my own eyes. On one of these visits, I met Kamal and had my perspective on the power of purpose changed forever.

Our group came across Kamal during our travels through the Nuba Mountains. He was a Sudanese leader fighting daily from his mountain hideout during the civil war in that country. Tragically, he had been tortured by the opposing forces in North Sudan for his Christian faith. They had tied him down on the hot rocks in the baking sun and left him to die. He was so badly burned he lost his hands and feet and could no longer walk. So, he scooted on his backside from place to place. He was sitting low to the ground looking intently up at us when our group met him. We were amazed to discover not only was he a man of faith but even through his capture and torture, he never denied his faith in Christ.

As we gathered around Kamal, my daughter, Carter, who was traveling with our group, asked him, "How can we pray for you?" His response: "Pray that I can complete the purpose God has for my life." Kamal clearly understood the power of purpose, and his one request was *Please pray that I can complete my God-given purpose.* His request wasn't for healing or his family or the war; it was for completing his purpose. He obviously knew his purpose and just wanted to complete it! What a great example of the power of purpose in our lives and in our organizations. As a postscript (see before and after photos), after our visit and return home, we were able to get Kamal much-needed surgery, and he actually walked out of the hospital following surgery in 2010 and continued fulfilling the purpose God had called him to accomplish.

After powerful eye-opening personal encounters like the one we had with Kamal, James and I launched Open Eyes in 2008. Open Eyes is a nonprofit organization that accelerates sharing the message of Jesus Christ to the most challenging places in the world. Our first initiative was the Mobile Messenger Program. We designed the program to provide motorcycles to the pastors and evangelists who, to reach people, had to make long trips on foot. With a motorcycle, they could cover more ground and get the message of God's love to those hard-to-reach villages.

But it's easy to tell you *about* Open Eyes. What can get lost in the story of the making of this organization is the passion behind it, the heart that stepped out into the unknown and dared to love deeply. Shortly after James accepted the invitation to help out in Lui, Sudan, he discovered the tremendous need of the people brought on by the daily suffering and loss they experienced. The work we continue to do with the organization reflects this passion to relieve pain and suffering. It was this heart for the people that inspired me to step into James's passion. And it changed me too.

Before James left for that initial trip to Sudan, he was a young man in search of something. Like you and me, he wanted to find his purpose in this world. When James accepted the invitation to get out of his comfort zone, he not only found a way to contribute and help people but also found purpose.

He'd tell me stories about the pastors he'd met on his travels and how hard they worked to bring a message of hope to people who needed it. These pastors and evangelists became mentors to him and lifelong friends to him and our family. I saw how they loved James as their own. But this really didn't surprise me, because James had a unique way of making everyone feel like family.

TWO LEADERSHIP INSIGHTS

James's story illustrates the value of two important leadership insights. The first one is this: Don't wait to lay the groundwork for an enduring legacy. You can start now. And it begins not with the externals in life but with what's inside of you.

The second is, the power of transformation can radically alter the course of your legacy. You and I can build our legacy each day. We build our legacy by caring for people, living with integrity, staying humble, and serving passionately. When people or business leaders decide to make significant changes in their approach to life and work, that transformation will undoubtedly capture the attention of others.

I've learned that if we can harness this kind of transformation, it can be used to incite incredible change in the lives of people, in corporate environments, and in whole communities.

START WITH A LEGACY MINDSET

Your legacy begins now. Though legacy is an accumulation of life and work, a *lasting legacy* is the sum of not only what you do but also who you are. What I mean by that is the type of person you are, the virtues you possess, and the character you cultivate.

Transformational leaders begin with a legacy mindset. They must not fall into the trap of barreling through life and work, hoping that their achievements will amount to something. I've seen too many leaders take that approach and then have to deal with the problems it produces. Instead, leading with the end in mind forces you to consider the reason why you do things or make certain decisions.

TRANSFORMATION IS CONTAGIOUS

I watched James's life *transform* before my eyes. Here's what's fantastic about observing someone, especially someone you love deeply, experience such a profound change in their life: Transformation is contagious.

I find this to be true in an individual's life and also in the corporate environment. When people encounter a person or culture that stands out from the status quo, they not only take notice but also want to be part of it. It inspires further change in their lives, and it fills an environment with a kind of buzz that's infectious.

James was infectious in his passion and transformation. When people see that you've changed and that you passionately desire to make the world a better place, it ignites a fire in them as well.

LEADERSHIP DRIVEN BY A HIGHER PURPOSE

James didn't wait for someone to sketch him a roadmap on how to help the people in the villages he encountered. He knew what needed to be done, and he set about to do it.

The world will tell you how to live, what needs to happen in your life, and in what order. But you and I must make a choice whether we listen to the world or to another, more excellent voice. Will we embrace the status quo in our lives and in our businesses? Will we tolerate a corporate environment just because that's just the way the world works? Or will we seek another path?

I believe the world needs this new breed of leader. For years now, we've understood leadership to be influence. And I still believe that is true—to a point. But a leader is far more than just an influencer.

I suppose you could argue that an influencer does not need to possess virtuous qualities because influence can be both positive and negative. When we define leadership as influence, what are we really saying? Are we saying all you need to do in order to be a leader is influence a person in some fashion? Well, I suppose that is leadership to some extent. But transformational leadership looks much different than mere influence.

I want to suggest we expand our definition of leadership to include qualities I believe are necessities for positive transformation. The transformational leader

- begins with the person in the mirror

- pursues virtue and transparency

- is guided by something deeper than influence

- is compelled by a higher purpose

When James decided to make a difference in the lives of the people he encountered in Africa, for example, he did so because he knew it was the right thing to do. He was driven by a *higher purpose*.

ONE-ON-ONE

I wrote this book to encourage you that we don't have to live and work according to the traditional rules of the world. We can forge new paths in our personal lives and in our businesses, ways marked with the deep values that make life meaningful and give purpose to our vocations.

Our journeys look different, and that's okay. I've thought through my journey and considered the legacy I want to leave for those who come after me.

The legacy I want to leave is composed of the lessons I've learned through personal transformation. I've learned so much through my own spiritual transformation, observing my son's transformation, and living through an incredible cultural transformation in our business. This word "transformation" keeps popping up in my life, and I love it.

When I think of the values that have guided my life as well as our business endeavors, I think of principles like accountability, purpose, humility, stewardship, pursuing growth, excellence, and commitment. It's not rocket science, and these values are not new. But like anything in life, knowing the path and walking the path are different things.

We hear words like "humility" thrown around in our society all the time. Still, who among us strives to be genuinely humble in leadership—it's a difficult task. Likewise, stewardship and accountability challenge our vision for the future and our innate desire to do what we want. But the men and women I admire most are guided by values such as these.

Who among us doesn't want to leave a meaningful legacy for those who come after we're gone? As we continue to explore what it means to be a transformational leader, consider these questions. Maybe take a minute or two and jot down your answers to them in your journal. If you're not someone who journals, maybe chat with a friend, family member, or coworker over lunch about them.

Questions to Consider

1. If you didn't wake up tomorrow, what would your legacy be? (I know, it's a sobering thought.)

2. Is your legacy wrapped up in externals like achievements, business success, or cash? Or are you investing in something more valuable than all of that stuff?

3. We all face the same end. How will you be remembered?

WOULD YOU WANT TO WORK HERE?

Let's apply some of what we're discussing to the corporate business world so we can see how who we are as people translates to what we become as organizations.

I want you to imagine for a moment that a Fortune 500 company recently hired you. You're excited because you've read so many great things about the company; it possesses high values, it treats its employees well, and it's just a great place to work. Then you show up for your first day.

You meet your boss, who seems slightly annoyed that he has to show you to your office, and then he drops you off unceremoniously in the breakroom, where you're to meet with another employee who's going to show you the ropes. As you stand there holding a cup of coffee waiting for your tour guide, another young professional enters the breakroom and pours some coffee and notices you standing there looking lost and confused.

"First day?" she says as she pours her creamer into her coffee.

"Uh . . . yes. I—"

"Save it. And get used to it. A little piece of advice. You'll hear all about our company's *way* today, but it's lip service. Nothing more."

"But I thought—"

"Yeah, so did I," she says as she turns and looks at you. "I mean, I suppose it's the thought that counts, but the only person who's on your side around here is you. Sorry."

Your new colleague exits the breakroom, leaving you deflated.

Now, of course, this is a made-up scenario. Still, if you've been around corporate culture as long as I have, you know that it's not uncommon for companies to preach all about values and their corporate culture when reality looks completely different on the inside. There are also companies that don't even try to hide it. They're all about the bottom line; it's a cutthroat world, and you better get used to it.

But who wants to be part of either company? Who wants to work in a culture of fear and backstabbing and selfishness?

You see, an organization's culture is more than just something you and I read on a mission or vision statement. It's the shared, learned, and silent assumptions on which people base their views of reality.

Don't get me wrong. It's a good practice to write down your values for everyone to see. We post ours in the entryway and at other strategic locations on our corporate campus, as well as throughout the Coke facilities in all our territories. Displaying our values reinforces their importance and reminds teammates why they signed on in the first place. Visually seeing them matters, but if those values aren't shared and learned by the folks running the ship, then they're just words on paper.

CULTURE REFLECTS LEADERSHIP

It comes down to leadership. A leader's view of the world and what he or she values matters tremendously. It filters into the fabric of the company. And this is true in life, whether in families or on teams or with nonprofits and ministries. If individual leaders view the world through a lens of selfishness, greed, and pride, then that will reflect in their families and throughout their teams and spread among their followers.

We need a new breed of leaders who are willing to show empathy and admit when they're wrong, who are comfortable with transparency, who care for everyone no matter who they are, and who desire to make a lasting positive impact in their communities. This kind of leadership sets the tone for your organization, your sports team, and even your family.

Peter Drucker once said this now-famous phrase: "Culture eats strategy for breakfast." I agree. But I want to tweak that thought just a bit. I believe *culture eats everything*. If your culture resembles the fictitious scenario that I sketched out previously, then your company will eventually be consumed from the inside out.

But if you and I can learn to be comfortable with a transformational mindset and style of leadership, I believe the sky's the limit not only for our organizations but also for our lives in general. Think of this little book as a case study on the value of transformational leadership and what happens when one company's culture experiences radical transformation.

WORK IT OUT

We've covered a lot of lofty ideas so far. Before we go any further, let's sketch out the profile of a transformational leader. I mentioned a few characteristics earlier, but now let's put them all together. That way you can revisit this for a quick refresher.

TRANSFORMATIONAL LEADERS:

- **Live and promote a faith-based (Christian) worldview**: They believe God owns it all, and they will be held accountable for all that has been entrusted to them, including their business and the people it comprises. They live for a purpose beyond business success and follow their faith convictions, seeking to honor God in all they do.

- **Serve others**: They believe they have not been appointed to be served but to serve, and they seek always to elevate the needs of others above their own. Others might say that their family and business hierarchy are upside down.

- **Lead courageously**: They recognize and accept their responsibility to drive shareholder value for the organizations they lead, and recognize faithful stewardship mandates growth. They seek to grow profitably because where there is no margin, there can be no mission. They generously share their margin in creative, courageous, and contagious ways.

- **Model transparency, humility, and accountability**: They believe what is caught is often more important than what is taught, so for them, the leader often goes first. They lead with vulnerability and transparently admit when they do not have an answer or have misled others or made a mistake. They recognize they are under authority and walk humbly before God and others. They embrace accountability as a friend and give as well as receive it freely.

- **Foster a life-giving culture**: They foster a life-giving culture in their homes, families, and workplaces. They believe excellence honors God, and they pursue it in their personal and professional lives. They cultivate the conditions in which others can flourish and grow.

GOD IS UP TO SOMETHING

Before I wrap up this chapter, I want to make one more point. Well, it's not really a point; it's more like a confession.

My faith in God lies at the center of what I believe it means to be a transformational leader. I believe James's story illustrates what a heart on fire for God can do. It was God who changed James's goals in life and ignited him to serve the way he did in Africa.

His transformation from just a young man seeking a path to one impacting the lives of people half a world away is the Christian story. It's one of total transformation. It's one of forgetting yourself and serving others. It's one of courage and purpose.

You may be a Christ follower and totally get what I'm saying. If so, fantastic. I trust the rest of this book will inspire and challenge you to give your life, family, and business fully to God so that you can see what happens when we give him everything we have—our family, our relationships, our work.

If you're not a Christ follower, that's okay too! I believe with all my heart that these principles are universal and apply to everyone. Why? Because God wants what's best for his children—all things good come from him. So even if you're on the fence about the faith element of this book, I believe you'll find just as many nuggets that can help transform your homes and work environments into flourishing havens of goodness.

....

CHAPTER 2

BRUTALLY HONEST

Clients don't expect perfection from the service providers they hire, but they do expect honesty and transparency. There is no better way to demonstrate this than by acknowledging when a mistake has been made and humbly apologizing for it.

—Patrick Lencioni

But transformation? Servant leadership? I know what you're thinking. Those concepts sound radical to many leaders—too risky to change the status quo, right?

They are radical concepts that require leaders to make challenging decisions. These decisions begin with a *brutally honest* evaluation of yourself and your work environment. When it comes to transparency, I've learned three things that transformational leaders understand.

First, they understand they must be accountable for their influence. This means they approach their life and work as a steward, someone who's been entrusted with a great gift, and it's their responsibility to care for and nurture that gift.

Second, they must constantly evaluate their past in order to learn for the future. It helps no one to shut the door on the past. On the contrary, the past operates as a helpful guide in times of trouble. Now, don't get me wrong, we can't *live* in the past. That's unwise. But we can certainly sharpen our leadership by remembering it.

Third, they must understand the consequences of their choices. I mean, let's be real, poor choices usually catch up with you. If you let poor cultural choices fester in your work environment, it can bring catastrophic results. If you consistently make poor choices or exhibit selfish behavior in your personal life, it can hurt the people you love the most.

YOU ARE ACCOUNTABLE FOR YOUR INFLUENCE

Life is short. If we spend it spinning our wheels, just going through the motions, we'll miss out on everything that God has planned for us.

Sometimes, like my son James, you've got to step up and out and seize the opportunity when it comes your way. And sometimes, when the opportunity doesn't come your way, you've got to get out there and go searching; you've got to get in the mix of life and see what God is doing and discover your part in it.

The point is, you can't sit back and watch life pass you by.

Here's a great verse from the Bible to think about: "Awake, you who sleep, arise from the dead, and Christ will give you light" (Eph. 5:14, NKJV). This verse is a personal wake-up call to me. Each time I read it, I have to ask myself again if I am living life asleep. Am I living my life on purpose, or am I settling for the status quo? Am I just going through the motions at work and with my family, or is there a deeper meaning behind it all?

Those thoughts hit me like a freight train. They remind me about that day sometime in the future when I stand before God, and he asks me, "Frank, what did you do with all that I gave you? What did you do with that company and people I entrusted to your care?"

The reality of the gifts God has given me, along with the responsibility I have to steward those gifts, hits me time and again with profound clarity. What am I doing with this tremendous gift, this awesome responsibility of leading the wonderful people at Coca-Cola Consolidated?

REEVALUATE WITH TOUGH QUESTIONS

I started to reevaluate my life, leadership, and legacy in my late thirties and early forties. I began to ask tough questions about my faith and my work. And I came to this conclusion: God owns it all. What am I going to do with it?

It's a question of accountability.

"Now hold on, Frank. What do you mean, God owns it all? Don't you have shareholders to consider?"

You are absolutely right. Let me explain.

GOD OWNS IT ALL

Don't let that heading scare you. It's simply stating a reality I like to live by. Of course, as a businessman, I clearly understand my responsibility to shareholders and want to generate great results for them. But at the highest level, this world is God's and everything in it. He created it, so he owns it—all of it.

In the Old Testament book of Psalms, the poet-king David writes, "The earth is the Lord's and everything in it, the world, and all who live in it, for he founded it on the seas and established it on the waters" (Psalms 24:1, NIV). Then there's the verse in Deuteronomy 10:14 (NIV): "To the Lord your God belong the heavens, even the highest heavens, the earth and everything in it." And there's this little pearl from the New Testament book of James: "Every good and perfect gift is from above, coming down from the Father of the heavenly lights, who does not change like shifting shadows" (James 1:17, NIV). You get the picture, right? When I say that God owns it all, this is what I mean. I believe that God as Creator of the universe owns it all because he created it all. That doesn't mean we just sit back and let things fall apart. No, he wants us to steward his kingdom. Twenty years ago, when we finally realized this truth, our attitude and action toward giving transformed, and so did our lives and our business.

As a businessman, I understood what accountability meant as it related to shareholders for the growth, health, and value of the company I was leading. And, from a spiritual perspective, I understood that I was accountable for how I lived my life before God. But I didn't understand accountability as it related to the influence and impact the company God had entrusted me to lead was having for Christ.

What did it look like to lead our company in a way that not only pursues excellence in its products but also excellence in its community engagement? What did it look like to serve not only the financial needs of our employees but their spiritual ones as well?

What did it look like to give our time and resources in a genuinely sacrificial way? I didn't know the answers to these questions, but I knew that I wanted to find out. I wanted to live life on purpose, and I wanted that purpose reflected in my work.

One thing that really inspired me was something I remembered the great evangelist Billy Graham saying: "The next revival in America is going to occur in the workplace." I think Dr. Graham was on to something. The experts say seven out of ten people don't attend church. But I can venture a good guess that those seven people who don't go to church show up on Mondays for work.

If you think about the workplace the way Rev. Graham suggested, the workplace *matters*. And if the workplace matters, then companies matter. And what we do in our place of business matters. The workplace doesn't have to be a place we dread. It can and should be a place devoted to a purpose, a place where we don't simply "clock in" and "do our time," but a place where we engage in meaningful work with people we care about and for a cause we believe in.

YOUR STORY MATTERS

After I asked myself some hard questions, I took a walk down memory lane and considered my story: my childhood, my influences, my values, things like that.

Like it or not, our purpose in life is wrapped up in our entire life's story. In order to determine why you're here and what you're supposed to do, you also have to consider who you were, who you are, and who you're becoming.

My story helps me understand where I came from and the factors that shaped me. When I look back, I can see that early in my life my mother and father, at different times and during different circumstances, planted seeds of transformation in my life. It was those seeds that produced a willing faith.

Over the past twenty-one years, I've witnessed seeds of faith grow and mature in our business. It's taught me that transformation doesn't just happen overnight; it is cultivated over time.

A good practice for any leader is reflecting on the past. Go ahead and set this book down and fire up your favorite dictation app or grab your favorite journal. Record or jot down the key events of your past. Who influenced you the most early in your life? What experiences shaped how you do your job or how you parent or how you run your business now? And don't forget to include your biggest mistakes and triumphs, those come in handy too. Later on, we'll do something with all of this info you're recording.

Now, if you'll allow me, I want to invite you into my past and show you some of the key points that shaped and inspired me to pursue a transformational type of leadership.

A BRIEF HISTORY OF
COCA-COLA CONSOLIDATED

In the introduction, I noted that Coca-Cola was invented in 1886 when John Pemberton stirred up the first batch of Coca-Cola in a drug store in Atlanta, Georgia. By 1891, another pharmacist in Atlanta, Asa Candler, had acquired all rights to the business for a total of twenty-three hundred dollars. In 1892, he then formed what is now known as The Coca-Cola Company. Under Mr. Candler's leadership the fountain beverage was being sold in and around the South when two fellows from my hometown of Chattanooga, Tennessee, got a great idea: to put Coke in glass bottles and franchise the system.

In 1899, these two gentlemen, Mr. Ben Thomas and Joseph Whitehead, traveled to Atlanta to meet with Mr. Candler. They talked him into selling them the franchise rights to bottle Coke for the entire U.S. for $1. Those rights were in perpetuity. The two Chattanooga lawyers negotiated a great deal with Asa Candler, and the business began to spread across the nation.

Suddenly, small Coke manufacturing and distribution operations sprung up all over the country, from California to New York. In the early days, the manufacturers produced one six-and-a-half-ounce returnable glass bottle of Coca-Cola—one at a time. They were delivered to customers by horse-drawn buggies. This was happening all over the country at the turn of the twentieth century.

The two Chattanoogans, Thomas and Whitehead, later teamed up with another fellow from Chattanooga, John T. Lupton, and they began to sell these franchises to family and friends.

My great-grandfather, J. B. Harrison, lived in Chattanooga

during this time. He started our first Coca-Cola franchise in Greensboro, North Carolina, in 1902. Soon after that, other franchises were opened in Raleigh, Winston-Salem, and High Point. The Charlotte franchise was also started in 1902 by the Snyder family. Similar deals were being negotiated all over the U.S., and by the early 1900s there were approximately a thousand Coca-Cola bottlers. Separate, private, family-run operations making, selling, and delivering one product and one package: six-and-a-half-ounce returnable glass bottles of Coca-Cola.

In the early 1970s the possibility of evolving federal regulations made us consider the benefits of becoming a publicly traded company. Add to this that we anticipated bottler consolidation—meaning, we knew some of the other Coca-Cola bottlers may elect to sell their businesses. Coke bottlers usually sell the company when there's not a family member to take it forward. We thought it made sense to raise capital to buy some of these companies.

Over the years, Coca-Cola Consolidated continued to grow and expand. By the time I joined the business in 1977, we had grown from a small business to an $80 million company. Our Coke franchises were centered in North Carolina and grew steadily. The brands sold by our company in the late '70s included Coke, Fanta, Sprite, Mellow Yellow, and Fresca. As we moved into the 1980s, the business ballooned with internal growth and external growth through the acquisition of other Coca-Cola bottlers.

On the internal side, The Coca-Cola Company did a great job of cranking out new brands and acquiring others. For example, in the '80s and '90s we added brands like Diet Coke, Cherry Coke, Dasani, and Powerade, pushing our stock-keeping unit (SKU) count to over one hundred items.

On the external growth side, we acquired other Coke franchises. You've heard the saying that only around three to five percent of family companies make it beyond three generations. Well, after a number of the Coke franchises had reached a hundred years of age, just as we predicted, the third generation began thinking about selling, or there were other family issues that brought about the sale of their companies. We were blessed to acquire a number of these family Coke operations.

From the 1980s to today our company now covers parts of fourteen states and the District of Columbia. At the moment, we sell over seven hundred million eight-ounce cases annually of the greatest products in the world, and our portfolio contains over three hundred brands and flavors. Our team of over sixteen thousand employees makes, sells, and delivers our beverages to almost twenty percent of the U.S. population, and our revenues are over $5 billion as of 2020.

It's humbling to think about how it all started, and how it's grown. I wake up each day feeling beyond blessed. It's funny, because some people still think we just sell Coca-Cola. They don't know about the three hundred brands and flavors. Once, a friend of mine told me she stopped drinking our products. What she meant was she had stopped drinking Coca-Cola.

"Do you drink water?" I asked her.

"Yes," she replied.

"Do you ever drink Dasani Water, Smart Water, or Vitamin Water?" I continued going down the list of Coca-Cola waters, juices, teas, coffees, energy drinks, sports drinks, milks, soft drinks, and all the incredible brands that we sell.

"I see," she said with a wry smile. She got the point.

Even though we've grown into something many of us never dreamed about, I still love looking back on how it all began. We should never close the door on the past, even on past mistakes. Instead, we should let it inform our growth in the future.

THE SHAPE OF MY EARLY LIFE

Now that you have a brief sketch of our business here at Coca-Cola Consolidated, I want to turn to the people who shaped me the most early in my life. Previously, I recommended taking a few moments and mapping out your own history, ups and downs, and influences. How'd that go? What's taking shape along your timeline? Is there a pattern of good, bad, and ugly? That's how it is with so many of us, so don't get discouraged if that's the way of it. Keep going!

And don't forget: Be honest about it all. There's no shame in owning up to your past. And there's nothing wrong with finding encouragement in the good memories as well.

Whenever I talk to folks at events or in meetings, I'm often asked how did I, a fourth-generation kid, end up in this Coca-Cola business? Well, here goes.

I was born in 1954 to Sue and Frank Harrison. Around that same time, my mother attended a Billy Graham crusade in Chattanooga, Tennessee, and gave her life to Christ. It wasn't long before my parents were following two very separate paths in life. By the time I was two years old, my father no longer lived at home. Our family unit was my mother, two sisters, and me in the middle.

Because my mother was one of nine children, we were surrounded by family and all that comes with grandparents, aunts and uncles, and lots of cousins. Our weekends were filled with yard games, good food, and church. As I got older, I spent many hours working alongside my grandfather, a former sheriff in Hamilton County, on his dairy farm. Some of my greatest memories were made on those long hot summer days baling hay and doing other chores.

My mother believed in the value of hard work and made sure my sisters and I were never idle. She loved to remind us that "Idle time is the devil's workshop." Get the picture? She kept us busy. But the greatest thing I learned from her was to love and live for Jesus. The person who literally gave me life is the one who led me to eternal life by leading me to place my faith in Jesus Christ. She taught my siblings and me to trust the Lord, honor his Word, give to others, and forgive.

She modeled Christlikeness by always speaking positively about my father and praying for him. As a result, years later as a young man, my heart had plenty of room for him to be a part of my life. During my childhood I never realized how steeped in the Coke business my father was or what that meant or could mean for me. I was too busy being a kid, doing farm work, going to church, chasing after my girlfriend and now wife Jan (will get to that later), and hanging out with my family. I wasn't aware of any expectation to step into the business. But once I entered college, that all changed.

During college, my father began to talk to me about

becoming familiar with the Coca-Cola business. He suggested I check it out by working on a route truck the summer after my sophomore year. It was the first time I felt that I might have a part to play in the business. And so it was that I became part of a company started by my great-grandfather, Buck Harrison, in 1902. What a blessing!

Over the years my father and I built a strong and loving relationship. He was instrumental in helping shape my training and preparation for leadership in the company. I learned a lot from him. He was a visionary, not a day-to-day guy. And I have to admit, some of the things I learned were related to things *not* to do in life and business. But as you might already know, those are some of the best lessons to learn.

MY EARLY LESSONS

I spent my first eight years working in our Coca-Cola plants first on the production line and then at the route level. Eventually, I became a supervisor, a sales manager, and a manager of several branches and sales distribution centers. Finally, it was time to move to Charlotte, where our corporate office was located. I spent the first couple of years in Charlotte managing the Charlotte sales center and then moved over to our corporate office.

My prior eight years were spent learning the business at the operations level. In those formative years of learning the business, I was fortunate to work in an environment where I was surrounded by an incredible team of Coca-Cola people. We were all about supporting each other, being a team, and taking it to the competition. It was like being on an athletic team in high school. I enjoyed the competition and the camaraderie at the plant level.

At the corporate office, it was a different world. I never knew what corporate politics was because I didn't experience that at the branch level. It didn't take long to learn about all the political games the executives liked to play at the corporate office.

On top of my new learning curve, I discovered the management team was not happy about my arrival. I was the chairman's son, but he lived in Chattanooga, Tennessee, and wasn't very close to the day-to-day operations of the business. Remember, he was a vision kind of guy. But he still expected the leaders to perform and generate great results, and he held them accountable.

My initial job was to report to the president and CEO and learn the business at the corporate level. In other words, I was supposed to move in and out of various job responsibilities, learn the business, and prepare myself to lead the company in the future.

That was not well received by the management team, and they played quite a few hide-and-seek games with me. In other words, leadership tried to keep certain activities of the company and all the political behavior away from me.

The eighties was a time of go, go, go; drive consistent strong results no matter what you needed to do. *How* those results impacted our people and our culture wasn't the important thing. All that mattered was the bottom line, which in turn would drive the stock price up and result in higher compensation for management. This mindset created a short-term mentality throughout the organization to drive short-term results. And, as you might imagine, that led to an unhealthy culture and a lot of bad decisions.

The top leaders spent too much time focused on Wall Street's opinion of the company. After giving future projections and talking about the great growth opportunities at the company, they then had to deliver those results. That obviously is not a good place to be and not where management should be focused to deliver long-term value creation. Once you begin to deliver strong short-term results, you must continue to cycle them. The next quarter is a big challenge because you always need to outperform the prior quarter. And before you know it, a big problem develops. You just can't keep up.

Long-term strategy was squeezed out by the monthly and quarterly goals. And because of the pressure to deliver, the goals *had* to be reached—period!

At that time in our company's history, if you would have asked someone to state our mission statement, I'm not sure what they'd have said. But if our actions reveal what's really in our hearts, then perhaps in those times the goal was to "get what you can now and don't worry about the long term."

Of course, no one would say that. Without a clear purpose—a reason why you show up to work each day—people tend toward self-preservation.

SELFISH BEHAVIOR WILL CATCH UP WITH YOU

In addition to the emphasis on short-term quarterly performance, everybody was playing politics. And if you were caught sharing the inside scoop with me, you were either moved out of the company or moved to another location.

I'll never forget what happened to my good friend Umesh, whom I had met at Duke's Fuqua School of Business. Umesh is a soft-spoken, gentle man of slight build and deep integrity who was and still remains in a significant leadership role for the company. He informed me about much of the selfish behavior in the corporate office, so the "politicians" at the office very quickly and quietly moved him up to Roanoke, Virginia, to lead the transportation department. Wow, imagining Umesh in transportation was an interesting thought; it was a true fish-out-of-water experience for him as he was thrust into the role of leading a group of truck drivers who were each nearly twice his size and at times much more "colorful" in personality. Imagine the look on Umesh's face when, in his very first meeting, one of the truckers asked, "What do you know about trucks? Have you ever driven one?"

Politics is a very interesting thing. I don't think I really understand it today, but I saw it in action during those years at Coca-Cola Consolidated. It does not nurture growth; it destroys it. Politics makes it all about me, my pride, and my ego and doing whatever it takes to make me look good. And that obviously leads to many bad decisions, because they're based on what makes you look good, not what is good for the long-term health of the company.

As we all know, what goes up must come down. After several years of the company being run for the short term and for the stock price and for pride, things began to go south. With managers too focused on themselves and outperforming the last quarter's results, the company had built an unhealthy culture that could not be sustained.

———

I'll never forget going down to the Bahamas in the mid-1980s when my father was on vacation. I spent a couple of days with him and began to bring him up to date on the toxic culture, the political mess, and the direction in which the company was heading. It was a good discussion—my dad knew something had to be done.

Soon after I left, he called the current leader at Coca-Cola Consolidated and told him he was upset about the things that were happening at the company. During their phone conversation he also said, "My son, Frank, will be your boss before too long. If he were your boss today, he would fire you."

That comment did not do well for my relationship with our current leader. But it was clear to me, and eventually to my father, that we needed to make a change in leadership, which we did.

As I think back over those years, I'm grateful my father trusted me enough to believe the things I told him versus the self-protecting views of the management team. At that time, I was a young and inexperienced businessman, while the other leaders were seasoned politicians. My father's support spoke volumes to me about his trust in my leadership.

I am forever grateful for the three years I spent in that difficult political environment. The greatest lessons in business and life come during times of great difficulty. Learning what not to do has been more valuable to me over the years than learning what to do.

The learning what not to do lessons feel harder and sink in deeper and are more impactful to your management style. I would not replace those years for anything. I thank God for them and the tremendous impact they had on me.

ONE-ON-ONE

The Bible goes pretty far when it says rejoice and be glad when you encounter trials and tribulations. Why should we rejoice in hardships? According to the Bible, they strengthen us, they mature us, they develop us into the person God wants us to be. I love how *The Message: The Bible in Contemporary Language* paraphrases this very idea:

> *Consider it a sheer gift, friends, when tests and challenges come at you from all sides. You know that under pressure, your faith-life is forced into the open and shows its true colors. So, don't try to get out of anything prematurely. Let it do its work, so you become mature and well-developed, not deficient in any way. (James 1:2–4)*

That was clearly my experience during those difficult years. Without them I would not have understood corporate politics, stock price compensation, the short-term view, the value of integrity, or the value of a purpose-driven culture, which we'll get into very soon.

In 1994, the board of the company appointed me chief

executive officer. By this time, thanks to the great work of our new president/COO, Jim Moore, the difficult management team had been replaced, and the company was restructured. It took several years to clean up the mess, but the company began to move in the right direction, which would continue under the strong and steady leadership of Bill Elmore. During his twelve years as president/COO and several business cycles during that timeframe, I was thankful to have Bill in that seat as the transformation of the company continued.

I've always said I was not ready for all the responsibility of becoming CEO of Coca-Cola Consolidated at the age of thirty-eight. But for as much as I needed to learn in my new role, there was one thing I understood very clearly. It wasn't my company; it was God's. It's as if God said to me, "Frank, someday you are going to be held accountable for the influence and impact this company has for *good*, for *God*, and for *growth*."

I understood accountability for myself and my own life before God, and I understood accountability before our shareholders for the growth, health, and value of the business. But accountability before God for the *influence* and *impact* of our company? Well, I wasn't sure what to do with that. Today, I refer to this as my wake-up call at Coca-Cola Consolidated. It was an important time, a transition time, for our company.

Not knowing what to do about this new calling, I did what you do when you don't know what to do. You do what you know you should do, and that is read the Bible, seek God's wisdom and direction, pray a lot, obey God, and wait until you know in what direction to move.

As I was trying to do those four things—*Read, Pray, Obey, Wait*—things began to happen.

WORK IT OUT

Okay, take a big deep breath. That's a lot of Coca-Cola Consolidated and Frank history. But I shared it for a reason. Well, two reasons actually. The first is to show you how important it is and what you can learn about yourself and your decisions when you spend just a few minutes and write them down.

The second reason is to show you the scope of my story and the challenges we faced when I came into a leadership position at our company.

Well, what the heck, here's a third reason. Part of my story is my wake-up call from God. It was a realization that I was accountable for my position of leadership. All of the assets, people, and programs he'd entrusted me with? Yeah, I was responsible to *him* for those things. That lesson alone, for me, was worth its weight in gold.

How about you? Since you're in note-jotting or dictating mode, here are three more questions for you to work out:

1. How might personal accountability to God for your organization influence and change the way you lead your organization and even your family?

2. Now that you've sketched out your own history, look for the road signs, the big decisions or events that shaped you. Ask yourself, "Where is God guiding me with

this?" and "What is he asking of me now?" Be honest with your answers. Sometimes the path markers are very clear, but we lack the courage to heed them.

3. In my story, it was evident that the status quo of doing business had to change. We lacked a healthy vision as a company. Ask yourself, and be honest, "Do I lack a compelling vision for my organization, for my family?" Too often we fail to ask vision and mission questions of our families, but that's a mistake. Families without a purpose will get pushed along by the slightest wind. But if you set your sails for a precise direction, you will, with God's help, reach those distant shores.

BONUS ROUND

When I reflect on my life like this, I review all the connecting points that made a difference, and it makes me thankful for the lessons I've learned. It also shows me to be on the lookout for opportunities to be a seed planter in the lives of others. People and experiences planted seeds in my life as a young man and businessman all along the way.

I think of my mother, Sue. She lived a pretty simple life in so many ways. She gave her life to Christ through a Billy Graham crusade, and but for her response, well, I might not even be writing these words. She planted a lot of seeds in my life—like hard work. I can smile at it now, but I have to admit lifting those scratchy bales of hay got the best of me some days. I'm sure my mom is smiling now at these words.

She planted the seeds of family and gathering as a family.

I'm sure it was uncomfortable for her at times to come to those gatherings without her husband, but she wanted extended family experiences for me and my sisters. And she planted the seeds of church, the Bible, and the good news of Jesus, who wanted a relationship with me. The fervent chords of those hymns still echo in my soul today. She didn't have to, but she planted the seeds for my father, and that was but one small mustard seed that, like the hymns, echoes thousands of times over.

Do you know the story of the mustard seed? Jesus liked that story and used it. The mustard seed, he said, is one of the smallest seeds ever, yet "when it has grown it is larger than all the garden plants and becomes a tree so that the birds of the air come and make nests in its branches." Mustard seeds become so much bigger and so much more productive than anyone could ever imagine. I guess that's part of the power of recognizing the seeds that have been planted in your life.

Seeds are funny things. You prepare the soil, maybe put in a little manure, plant a hard-shelled object, cover it up, cultivate it, and water it, and you yield something totally unlike that seed. It's the principle of sowing and reaping. You sow singularly but reap in multiples. But the waiting between the sowing and the reaping can seem like forever.

For the Bonus Round, jot down the people in your life who have planted seeds along the way. Take some time to text or call them, write them a note of thanks, and then write down the names of people for whom you can be a seed planter.

....

CHAPTER 3

THE POWER OF A TRUTHFUL ORGANIZATION

*Personal leadership is the process of keeping your vision
and values before you and aligning your life to be
congruent with them.*

—Stephen Covey

What does it mean for an organization to be truthful?

I believe transformational leaders seek to build truthful organizations. Truthful organizations are founded upon purpose and well-communicated and consistently modeled values. I want to spend some time looking at this idea of purpose and introduce the critical task of knowing, articulating, and living your principles. By the end of this chapter I want you to be excited about crafting your own purpose statement and establishing guiding principles for your organization and family.

In creating a healthy, purpose-driven culture, leaders must begin with establishing core values that inspire team (and family!) members. But as necessary as this step is, it's not enough to write these values on the wall. *These principles must become part of the fabric of the company.*

"But, Frank, how do you do that?"

"I'm glad you asked. It all starts with your purpose."

LIFE ON PURPOSE

For me, the idea of purpose stems from my faith in God. Purpose for me is an all-encompassing notion that relates to my spiritual life (first and foremost), my personal life (my family), and my vocational life (Coca-Cola Consolidated). When I share the importance of purpose with others, some of them look at me kind of strange. They simply don't understand how knowing your purpose in life can relate to work. I can sit here now and tell you that this idea makes clear sense to me. But early on in my business career, business was business. I didn't think about how to incorporate my faith into my vocation; those were different parts of my life.

But I was wrong. God blessed me with a family and with the ability to work and build a business. Not only was I responsible and accountable for my private life, but God also wanted me to work for him in my place of business. Having a purpose in my personal and family life carried over into my business life. Breaking down the silos between personal and vocational life was a revelation. When you view purpose the way God views it, your whole world changes.

When this wake-up call about accountability hit me square in the heart over twenty-five years ago, I had no idea what it meant. I was growing in my faith, had a growing family at home, and was leading a growing business. All of that coupled with my personal reflections led me to a point where I realized I was not an owner of anything but had been entrusted to steward myself, my family, and my business for good and for God's glory. So, I gathered some leaders, and we began to pray about how we could lead the company with greater accountability before God. We asked the question, What does it look like to honor God with this business?

The answer? Purpose.

Purpose answers the question, Why are we here? I believe part of our purpose is to love and honor God with the gifts he's given us. And I also believe that to honor God with what he's entrusted to us, we need to be intentional about how we live our lives. Author Kevin McCarthy says, "Being on-purpose requires commitment and effort, but it creates freedom and opportunity. Sliding through life unfocused leaves you caught between chaos and confusion."[3] If you're not living life on purpose, he says, then you're just people pleasing. And who wants to do that?

We began asking ourselves the question, Why are we here? When we started to answer the question, we discovered that when you nail down a purpose for your company or any entrepreneurial endeavor, you take the first step at creating your company's culture.

At Coca-Cola Consolidated, our culture is our purpose. You'll see why that statement makes sense in a moment. Once we figured out what our purpose was as a company, we wrote it down; we put it on one sheet so employees could easily read it. We also felt it was important enough to give it prominence throughout our entire corporate office and throughout all of our production and distribution facilities in the field. It reads:

OUR PURPOSE

To Honor God in All We Do

To Serve Others

To Pursue Excellence

To Grow Profitably

It's not some overly impressive idea. It's simple, clear, and easy to remember. And best of all, it acts as a guardrail for our entire company. We use it to measure ideas.

"Does this idea contribute to our purpose?" we ask.

"Does it help us serve others better?"

"Does it honor God?"

When you can see and read your purpose day after day, it does something to you. It gets into your DNA and reminds you why you're here.

So why are you here? Why is your business here? Have you ever asked those hard questions?

Let's look at these questions, first, as they relate to a company's culture. And then I'll offer some thoughts on how we can apply this concept to our personal lives as well.

HOW CULTURE AND PURPOSE RELATE

I like to tell folks that our purpose is our culture, and our culture is our purpose. Earlier, I told you a little about our company's history. We certainly had a mission back then, but as I said, it was self-centered and all about being the best in the short term. Over time, we realized there is something more inspirational, more motivational, more eternal to be pursued in this life. And it is purpose.

But what do we mean when we say, "Purpose is our culture or culture is our purpose"?

We believe purpose drives everything we do, in both our personal and professional lives. It's the *why* behind our actions. Simon Sinek reminded the world to start with why. The why is your purpose. It's what drives you.

Have you ever asked yourself the why questions? Like, why are you in business for yourself? Or why did you choose the college you attended? Or why did you move to that city at that time in your life? There's a why behind each and every one of those decisions. Or at least there should be.

When we talk about the why as it relates to our company's purpose, we believe it is something greater than ourselves. I can tell you the numbers behind our company's day-to-day production, and I can tell you what we do—we manufacture, sell, and distribute Coca-Cola products to businesses located in certain areas of the country. But *why* do we do that?

I believe that our why, our purpose, comes directly from our faith. God wants us to do good work and to honor and glorify him in all that we do. That's our baseline; that's our purpose. And that baseline is the bedrock of the three other pillars of our purpose: to serve others, to pursue excellence, and to grow profitably. Every decision we make stems from that purpose. It guides how we go about our business. And it establishes a bar of accountability that transcends every person in the company, from manufacturing to distribution, to the executive team and our board of directors. When your purpose drives your decision making in such a complete way, your entire organization begins to take on that purpose. It saturates everything you do. And before you know it, your culture reflects your purpose. That's how you create a purpose-driven corporate culture.

WHY YOUR CULTURE IS IMPORTANT

I once heard that influence can rise, but culture always falls. That means anyone in any position of a company can influence another—someone who serves under them, their manager, and even their CEO.

But a company's culture falls from the top. Like it or not, it's the responsibility of the top leaders of an organization to establish a culture, and that culture will either be one in which people feel safe and empowered, or it will be one in which people feel threatened, unsafe, and fearful to use their abilities to contribute to the corporate purpose.

If culture falls, then I want it to first fall from God. And I want God to inform everything about our business. When he does, the leadership guidance doesn't come from me. It comes from something *beyond* me.

At Coca-Cola Consolidated, we believe that culture is the most important thing. And I believe that is true for any organization, profit or nonprofit. It's the most important thing because your culture is you and your VP and your plant manager and your route driver and your sales manager and your marketing director. Culture is your people. And when your people get passionate about their purpose, then the actual day-to-day work takes on new significance. It becomes a thing of joy rather than what can often be a thing of drudgery.

Remember, culture eats everything. By that we mean it's the most important thing in your business, and when you get it right, people get inspired and motivated about the culture, and great things come forth.

I feel as though many organizations don't know what their culture is. They *say* they do; they repeat a mission statement, but it seems to be just words that get lost in the day-to-day workflow. A great culture is attractive. People want to work in a great culture. I love to welcome new employees from other companies and hear their reactions to our culture.

One of the main reasons Dave Katz, our current president and chief operating officer, joined our company was our purpose-driven culture. He was doing very well at a much larger company but was attracted by our culture. Our president and chief operating officer before Dave was Hank Flint. Before he joined our company, Hank was the co-leader of one of the largest law firms in Charlotte at the time. After a great deal of thought and prayer, Hank felt called to our company.

"I *had* to come here, Frank," he said. "I had no choice."

I believe culture is all about how we do business and how we treat people, how we behave, and how we do life together. A great culture attracts great people to your company, and it also retains them. You know a great culture when you are in one.

But what makes a great corporate culture? Easy: purpose.

ONE-ON-ONE

Why is Coca-Cola Consolidated here on this earth? That's the question I asked myself over and over again early on as I was seeking God's direction. When you and I talk about purpose, we can talk about it in two ways. First, there's our overarching purpose for existing on this earth—you know, the big-picture type of purpose, like what we use in our purpose statement discussed earlier. We can also be talking about our vocational purpose—you know, what God wants us to do with our personal gifts and abilities.

What's comforting is that the concept of purpose is a biblical principle. You can find a great verse around the idea of an overarching purpose in life in Jeremiah 29:11:

> *"For I know the plans I have for you," declares the Lord.*
> *"Plans to prosper you and not to harm you.*
> *Plans to give you hope and a future."*

This verse came from the prophet Jeremiah to the people of Israel when they were struggling in captivity, living in a strange land and desperate for hope. They had dreams of returning home, but God had other plans for them—plans better than the ones they had for themselves. It proves that no matter what the circumstance, God has a plan and purpose for every circumstance and for every person. Bible teachers tell us that each person is called uniquely and created uniquely, and this gives us our deepest sense of purpose.

Isn't it comforting to know that God created us with a special purpose in mind? He gave you specific abilities to use for his glory here on planet earth. Do you know what yours are? An easy way to determine your unique calling is to ask yourself what you are passionate about. When your passion for something intersects with your gifts and abilities, then you're on the right path!

Psalm 16:11 (NIV) says, "You make known to me the path of life." God doesn't hide your calling from you. He wants you to experience the depth of meaning and purpose in this life.

I'm no expert in biblical teaching, but I can offer you this little nugget. When you live life in the confidence of your unique abilities and you experience profound purpose and meaning, it helps you prioritize and schedule your life. Just like a business, if you know the why, then you know the most important thing. You can say no to opportunities that might sound good but do not align with your why. You can fill your days and focus your attention on the things that resonate with your why, with your purpose.

I wanted to share my thoughts on purpose because it was

integral to our company's journey. Back in 2010, we figured if an individual could express a God-given purpose, then maybe our company and its sixteen thousand teammates could express and pursue a corporate purpose. We went to work on our corporate purpose—word by word. After much thought, prayer, and discussion, the final version emerged. I shared it earlier, but it bears repeating: Our Coca-Cola Consolidated purpose today is to honor God in all we do, serve others, pursue excellence, and grow profitably. This corporate purpose drives our company culture.

WORK IT OUT

"But, Frank, what about all this God talk? I mean, I know you're a man of faith and all of that, but we're talking about businesses. Can you really talk like this in this secular world of ours?"

Good question! I'm glad you asked. Yes, it's true our purpose statement is God-centric. We aim to honor God in all we do. And yes, people do say, "Wow! That brings up the God question at a public company. Can you talk about God at your company?"

To which I reply, "Of course you can, and it doesn't matter whether the company is public or private." If you want to talk about your faith at work, you have every legal right to do so. You can have a Bible study at work, and you can even pray at work. All that is completely good and legal. Of course what you cannot do is discriminate against or harass someone because their faith is different from yours. And you also need to be sure to try to accommodate their religious practices when you can. These rules are not only the law but also right and how we should act in order to honor God in all we do.

From time to time, if I am sharing my faith with a group of employees, I will remind our folks, "This is what I believe, and if you believe something different, that is all well and good. We will never, ever discriminate against or harass anybody for any reason at Coca-Cola Consolidated." Our people represent different faith backgrounds, and some folks have no faith background. If someone is an atheist and says they don't believe in God and therefore they don't have to honor God, we will say, "Okay, but you do have to sign up for our values." We don't push our faith onto anyone, but we do expect our employees to be honest, ethical, and moral.

Our values-based culture has been a continual work in progress over the past twenty years. We are committed to loving and serving our people no matter their faith background. When we say we will honor God in all we do, we are simply saying we will do our best to live out our values.

"Honor God" is a banner of accountability for us. It is out here, up high. We look up to it and do our best to live it. We have a similar banner around market share growth. It is simply labeled "10 in 10." It means we aspire to grow ten market share points in ten years. Having a banner of accountability serves as a reminder to everyone in our company; we never forget our values, and when your values stay front and center, your company culture will reflect it.

Now it's your turn. Hopefully you understand how important it is to operate your business and your life with a clear statement of purpose. Ours isn't rocket science. It's simple but clear, and it helped us formulate the core values we want to be known for as a company.

Here's your homework for this chapter. Commit to spending some quality time with your team to discuss your purpose statement. Schedule some brainstorming sessions to get all the ideas on the table. It will take some time, but it will be time well spent, especially when you consider how much of your company's transformation hinges on your purpose statement. Need some inspiration? Then hey, feel free to jot ours down as a reminder of what you're going for. Or do a quick Google search for other organizations that you love and respect.

Here's what you're going for with your purpose statement:

1. Simplicity

2. Clarity

3. Inspiration

I think you'll be surprised at the freedom that comes from investing the time necessary to iron all of this out. Once set, then you can get to work on establishing your core values, which we'll dive into next.

CHAPTER 4

....

BREAK THE CYCLE

Action speaks louder than words but not nearly as often.

—Mark Twain

B reaking the cycle doesn't just happen by wishing it to happen. Breaking anything requires action. You can't break something, like a board or a window, by staring at it—unless of course you're one of those superhero-type people with a cape. You break something with decisive action, like throwing a ball through the glass or taking a sledgehammer to the board.

We didn't throw a ball through glass, but we did a whole lot of praying. And we did a whole lot of trusting God as we took one step at a time toward total culture transformation.

Thanks for hanging with me all the way to chapter four. I'm honored to be able to sit with you and tell you our story and some of the lessons we've learned along the way. In the last chapter we talked a lot about purpose. Did you put in some work and craft your own purpose statement? Great! That's not an easy task, and it takes more time than people realize.

When you discover the power of a truthful organization, amazing things are sure to follow. If you remember, in chapters one and two, I sketched a bit of my personal story and the history of my family's involvement in the Coke business. Our culture wasn't always like this. It was a mess. And it didn't provide our team members a safe space to thrive in their callings. Establishing a purpose statement was a first step to breaking the cycle of politics and short-term, selfish behavior in our corporate culture.

If you have a few minutes, I want to share a few more decisions we made that helped break that unhealthy cycle once and for all. Early on in our transformation, my dear friend Bob Pettus, who was our VP of human resources, and I stumbled upon the most unlikely blessing for our entire company. You'll never believe it.

A CURIOUS PROPOSITION

One day, a friend and I were talking shop about life and our businesses, and he mentioned that he'd hired a chaplain in his manufacturing plant. At first, I was taken aback by this. It immediately got my wheels turning. Not only did they pull the trigger on getting chaplains for his plant, but he said the team members embraced it. It was a good thing!

I remember thinking to myself, *Hmm . . . a chaplain in a Coke plant? Never done anything like that in over one hundred years, and it's got to be illegal. A public company with a chaplain? No way.*

I let the idea go.

But what was so powerful that day was the fact that my friend had planted a seed. There is great power in being a seed planter. You and I need to be seed planters in all that we do. We need to be intentional and plant all kinds of seeds and then get out of the way and give God time to water and fertilize. Once the seeds germinate, they produce good, godly fruit.

After the chaplain seed was planted, I kept running into chaplains over the next few months.

During that same timeframe, I received and accepted an invitation from our Mecklenburg County sheriff to visit his office. As I was walking around the sheriff's office during my visit, I passed an office with a placard above the door that read, "Chaplain."

"Sheriff, do you have a chaplain on site?" I said.

"Yes, we have a chaplain. It's been such a good thing too. Nobody has given me any grief."

Wow, I thought, *a chaplain in county government!*

Soon after, I visited with the football coach from a large public university, thanking him for their Coca-Cola business. And it happened again. Coach and I walked by an office with the word "Chaplain" on the door. Coach took a moment and introduced me to the chaplain.

A public university? I thought as we chatted. *Can they have a chaplain?* Well, obviously they can.

That seed my friend had planted weeks earlier was beginning to germinate.

AN UNLIKELY BLESSING

A few weeks later, I attended the Coca-Cola 600, a NASCAR race we sponsor in Charlotte. Right before the race there was a drivers' meeting in which announcements were made and various rules discussed. Right after the drivers' meeting, they held—you guessed it!—a chapel service. I noticed a number of the teams attended and many of them had—boom!—*chaplains*.

Well, I thought, *if I were going to speed around that track at 200 mph, I would definitely be at that chapel service.*

After running into all those chaplains over a six-month period, I realized the obvious: A lot of businesses and organizations use or employ chaplains. I wondered exactly what to do. What was God telling me?

I went back to work the next week and met with Bob. "Hey, Bob," I said, "I've been thinking . . . maybe we should look into this chaplain thing. It may not be that crazy of an idea after all."

After a good bit of debate about it, we decided to do a test in our Nashville Coke plant. We did our due diligence and hired professionally trained counselors who possessed counseling and seminary degrees. They are trained ministers and counselors who have five to ten years of workplace experience—true professionals.

After having our chaplains in place for about nine months in Nashville, we got a call from our human resources folks there.

"We know that this is kind of a test," they said, "but we're telling you right now that if you pull these chaplains, then we are going to have a revolt on our hands. It's incredible what they have accomplished. They are literally rescuing our people. Marriages are being saved. They helped get a kid out of jail and restored to his family. Suicides were prevented in a couple situations."

What a blessing!

There was actually someone on site now who could counsel, help, mentor, and coach our people through great difficulty in their lives. When a company's benefits include restoring your marriage, how do you measure that value? The return is powerful and eternal. Let me give you an example.

During the test period, one of our employees who found Christ through his close relationship with one of our chaplains passed away. His family didn't have a church and asked if they could have the funeral at the Coke plant. I didn't know anything about it, but they had the funeral at the plant, back at the loading docks. Several people's lives were changed for eternity.

After that we said, "Whoa, this is powerful! It's time to spread the chaplains throughout the company." These chaplains continue to have a profound impact on our people and our business.

AN IMMEASURABLE ROI

It is rare when I visit our Coke plants today that someone doesn't come up to me and say, "Thank you for our chaplains, they helped my family through a crisis" or "They helped put my marriage back together." The stories go on and on.

The beauty of the chaplaincy program is that our chaplains build lasting relationships with our people and *earn* the right to care for them when crises strike.

As our chaplains tell me, all of us are either in a crisis, just getting ready to go into a crisis, or just coming out of one. And that's when our chaplains do their best work. We've had chaplains from Corporate Chaplains of America for over twenty-one years now. Over those years there have been thousands of interactions with our teammates. We now have chaplains serving our sixteen thousand employees and their families in approximately one hundred facilities.

I am so thankful for these men and women and the positive impact they are having on our business. The return on our investment is immeasurable. In the last phases of writing this book, our nation and the entire world is battling the COVID-19 pandemic. I can't tell you how critical our chaplains are as they help sustain the spirit of our company during this crisis. They serve as a constant and critical source of encouragement during unprecedented times. When a true crisis emerges, we are blessed to have chaplains on our team and on site 24/7 to meet the psychological and spiritual needs of our team members.

———

The chaplaincy program was the beginning of a visible transformation that took place at Coca-Cola Consolidated. It was a key aspect of the great culture shift we witnessed in the company. The chaplaincy program helped us further understand how important establishing our purpose was to turning our culture around.

WHAT ARE YOU KNOWN FOR?

Breaking the cycle of the past takes an incredible amount of commitment from you and your team, but you can do it. It also requires a bit of risk taking—or perceived risk taking. For me, I never thought we'd be able to start a chaplaincy program. The thought never entered my mind. Why? Because of my preconceived notion that it wasn't legal. But it is! So, I perceived a problem that wasn't even reality. Nevertheless, we took the "risk," and it's paid wonderful dividends in terms of the health and morale of our company and the blessing of serving our employees and team members who flat-out love our chaplains.

In the previous chapter, I walked you through the importance of establishing a purpose statement. I explained how having a simple, clean, and inspirational purpose aids your decision making. That was certainly the case when it came time to pull the trigger on our chaplaincy program. It fit with our purpose, so it was a no brainer.

The chaplaincy program remains a strong example of the early seeds of transformation that basically took over our corporate culture. But in addition to our purpose statement and adding programs like our chaplaincy program, we also established a list of the values—some might call them principles—we wanted to be known for as a company. Let's dive into those values. As you read our list of values, take a few notes, either mental notes or in your journal (or journaling app), on what values resonate with you.

Or maybe our values will stir your creative juices, and you'll think of values more appropriate for you and your brand. That's great! The main thing to remember is established values help guide thinking and actions for you and your team members, and one of the first things you need to accomplish is getting the right set of values in place.

When we stick to solid values, take them to heart, and allow them to penetrate our daily lives, it's hard for any culture to remain unchanged.

VALUES TO LIVE BY

As I said earlier, we're not going to tell our teammates who God is; they've got to figure that out. And if they don't believe in God, well, that's their right and their business, but we do expect them to follow our values.

With that said, here's how it works for us. We believe we honor God by living out our ten values: accountability, consistency, courage and conviction, discipline, honesty and integrity, humility, morality, optimism, respectfulness, and supportiveness. We don't have the space in this book to go into every value in detail, but I wanted to list them here with a thought or two on each.

> **Accountability**: A commitment to be
> responsible for one's actions and results.
> How do we do that? By being willing to
> answer for what we do and say.

> **Consistency**: A harmony of conduct or
> practice in all matters. How do you do that?
> Doing the right thing time after time. You are
> dependable, valuable, trustworthy.

Courage and Conviction: The confidence and resolve to take actions based on a strong set of beliefs in the face of hardship. How? By taking a stand for what we believe in. Tell the truth, be bold, gain respect. Stand firm.

Discipline: Controlled behavior resulting from training and commitment. How? It's about body, mind, and spirit and bringing an orderly process to all our behavior. Stay focused on what's important. Make it a lifestyle, and develop routines like reading, time with God, and eliminating excuses.

Honesty and Integrity: Sincerity, truthfulness, and the firm adherence to a code of values. How? Always tell the truth, the whole truth, and do it consistently.

Humility: The quality of being humble. How? Focus on others more than one's self. Others first. The proud fall; God promises the humble will be exalted. Servant leadership leads to serving, leads to growth, leads to greatness. The idea of descending to greatness.

Morality: A system of ideas of good and right conduct. How? Practicing good, right behavior and keeping it clean.

Optimism: Exhibiting a "can do" attitude and emphasizing the positive aspects of a situation. How? Thinking positive—an upbeat positive attitude is contagious. As a person thinks, so is he.

Respectfulness: To treat others with high regard. How? Showing consideration and courtesy, and esteeming others.

Supportiveness: To serve as a foundation for others, to be an advocate. How? Helping, lifting up, and assisting others.

Remember, our purpose, "To honor God in all we do," operates like a banner of accountability. It's up there, we see it everywhere, and it serves as a reminder and a real challenge every day to live out our values.

This is how purpose and values work so beautifully together—by keeping everyone locked into the same mindset. Purpose inspires everyone with a goal beyond themselves, and values give them a roadmap on how to do it.

HONESTY MATTERS

I want to briefly hit a few values that impact our corporate culture so much: honesty/integrity, humility, and morality. The first value comes with a twin: honesty *and* integrity. Honesty stands as one of our most foundational values. If you don't get this one right, you're in big trouble. Your culture will have no credibility.

Someone once told me everyone at her company lies all the time. "They lie about everything," she said.

That is terrible, I thought. But oh, how common. If there is no truth, there is no trust. And if there is no trust, then there are no relationships. You and I know life and business center on the relationships we cultivate here on earth and with God above.

You and I have to learn to tell the truth, to stop exaggerating reality, to stop telling white lies. It's difficult. Trust me, I know. But you and I have to work at this one. I pray every day for help in being one-hundred-percent truthful. But what a difference it makes when an organization is truthful. Truth forces corporate politics to flee.

Occasionally I enjoy asking an audience, "How many of you have told a lie in the last week?" You'd be surprised at the varying responses. Once, I spoke to two hundred prisoners and asked them that question. I bet ninety-eight percent of them said they had told a lie in the past week. Now those were some truthful people.

Contrast that episode with, say, just about any business or church audience. When I ask them the same question, very few raise their hands and admit that they have told a lie within the last week. Can you believe it? And yes, I do call out the ones not raising their hand.

You can't skimp on honesty. Our culture at Coke expects us to be truthful with one another. You'd be surprised how freeing it is to admit it when you screwed something up or forgot to fill out a report. I'm reminded of this verse in Proverbs: "Whoever walks in integrity walks securely, but whoever takes crooked paths will be found out" (10:9, NIV).

The truth is way less stressful than lies.

SO DOES HUMILITY

Humility is the idea of putting the needs of others before your own, thinking of others before yourself, serving. Jesus told his followers that the greatest among them would be the servant.[4] The idea does not mean that if you want to be great, then serve. It actually redefines what greatness is. It's a countercultural idea.

Culture conditions us to equate greatness with winning; greatness equals status, greatness equals money, and so on. But Jesus viewed greatness with a completely different lens.

Humility, in the way of Jesus, entails rejecting the benefits that a position or a status might afford you. The humble person is the person seeking to serve their colleague. The humble person seeks to elevate others and will even sacrifice their own status if it means serving someone else.

Jesus showed us what true humility was when, the night before he was killed, he took off his robe and acted as the servant and did something completely countercultural: He washed his disciples' feet. It was such a scandalous act that one of his closest friends stood up to protest.

Humility is one of those difficult values to strive after. Because just when you think you've become humble, you're actually not. Humility is not a badge you achieve; it's a posture you cultivate—a way of life that you nurture through service.

Remember what happens to the proud—they fall. Maybe not immediately, but in the end, they will get the reward of pride. And it's not good, let me tell you. The famous British writer C. S. Lewis said this about pride: "A proud man is always looking down on things and people: and, of course, as long as you are looking down, you cannot see something that is above you."[5] Pride and humility—attitudes of heart-perspective. Instead of looking down on others, how can I get on my knees (figuratively, unless of course, you want to wash your team members' feet—which I actually recommend!) and serve my fellow team member? Keeping that perspective at the forefront of our minds will keep us in a posture of humility.

"But, Frank, how do you promote a culture of humility?"

"I'm glad you asked!"

Practically speaking, I think it begins with taking certain perks away for those in leadership roles. I know some reading this part might cringe, but don't worry, you'll get over it. This anecdote might seem trivial, but this is the kind of thing I'm talking about. Back in the '80s some of our key leaders had special parking spaces—you know the kind that are front and center, the kind in which you only have to walk a few steps to the front doors of the office building. Heaven forbid a person might have to walk too long in the rain!

You can imagine that those spaces were one of the first things to go. It's a small gesture, but I believe it speaks to the building of humility in our culture. It rids the air of this sense of entitlement. No one likes to work with an entitled leader. That's easy to say but tougher to live out. I believe cultivating an environment in which humility is prized over entitlement endears employees to their leaders and fellow colleagues. Removing entitlement-inducing extras for leaders can do wonders for your company's morale, but perhaps more importantly it paves the way for building true humility within the ranks of your company.

In Jim Collins's lifework *Good to Great*, he talks about the paradox of the Level 5 leader. This leader is defined by a paradoxical mix of humility and ambition. But the key is that the ambition they seek is not for themselves; it is for their company. At one point, Collins names President Lincoln as an example of one of our country's few Level 5 leaders. Why? Because he showed great humility in his quest to unite our country even at great expense. His ambition was for the country he served, not himself. The humble leader is the leader who will quietly go to any length to achieve the greatest outcome for the entity they guide.

VALUE MORALITY

Finally, there's morality. Morality covers a lot of ground, I know. Morality, for us, means understanding the difference between right and wrong. It's staying away from the edge so you don't fall in. It's doing the right thing no matter the cost. I think a story will make the point better than any definition I can give you.

Recently, I was visiting with one of our past Coke leaders for a discussion about how he was doing in his role with a new company. He was telling me about his first year with our company back in the 1990s. He started with us as a management trainee and, soon after, we sent him to one of our markets to become a route supervisor.

During his first week on the job, he was riding along with the delivery merchandising guy and stopped at a convenience store to deliver an order. When they entered the store, the manager used a racial slur not worth the ink to put on this page to refer to our new route supervisor who had announced, "I am the supervisor here today helping our delivery man."

"Well, you're not welcome in my store, and do not come back."

So, our new route supervisor left the store after the product was delivered and called his manager at the plant. His manager apologized for the incident and told him not to worry about it—they would talk when he and the delivery merchandiser returned.

At the end of the day our route supervisor returned to the plant, and there was his manager with a few other guys and a big pickup truck.

"Hop in," his manager said to him. "We're going to go pick up some product at a store."

As the route supervisor tells this story, he includes noticing his manager had a check in his hand, which he thought was unusual. They drove for a bit and pulled up to the account where the store owner earlier that day had called our new route supervisor every dirty word in the book. Our route supervisor wondered what was going on when his manager walked in and said hello to the store manager.

His manager then announced that he and his colleagues were going to pick up every case of Coca-Cola product in the store.

Referring to our new route supervisor who was standing nearby, his manager said simply and clearly, "Since my man is not good enough for you, then neither is Coca-Cola. We will take all our product and write you a check for it, and then we are out of here."

Our manager handled the whole situation with ease and professionalism. He just knew the *right* thing to do and did it.

———

You see, these core values work in unison with our purpose to honor God in all that we do. When we let these values guide our actions, it shapes our company culture. A culture is influenced by the actions of people. That's true in our country's culture too; how our leaders in office act trickles down and establishes how people treat one another and so on.

If a company does not institute core values, then they are actually instituting something very negative. They are telling the people who work there that they don't care about how you act; just get your job done. By not giving people a vision of your purpose, you're opening the floodgates for bad behavior.

Everything we do or don't do establishes the culture of a company. When you give people a purpose—a good purpose—it will transform their mindset and encourage them to strive to achieve that purpose. The result? An on-purpose culture.

ONE-ON-ONE

I hope by now you get the point. Breaking the cycle of short-term, selfish behavior requires action. And sometimes that action is hard. I'd like to share another program that's having a tremendous impact in our company. Well, it's hard to call it a "program." It's actually something completely volunteer based. It's our prayer and Bible study groups.

A growing number of prayer groups meet regularly through-out the company. I'm in one every Monday morning, and I make about eighty percent of the weekly prayer meetings. We pray for our people, their issues and problems. We pray for customers, suppliers, business deals, all sorts of things.

My prayer group started five years ago when we were working on a large acquisition. We needed plenty of wisdom and guidance, so I asked for prayer during one of our meetings. And I'm glad I did. I received a lot of peace from knowing that our company and our decisions were prayed over by members of our group. When things got off track, I wasn't too worried because I knew we'd given it to prayer. The impact of prayer over the next decade by our prayer groups versus the alternative, which is no prayer, is a powerful thought.

"But, Frank, you can't pray in the workplace. In this day and age? That's illegal! Right?"

"Thanks for the concern, but no, actually that's not right. It *is* legal. You can pray in the workplace."

A number of years ago I attended a Billy Graham CEO conference. I was part of a panel of six CEOs, and we were fielding questions from the audience. Someone asked, "Frank, what would I do if two people from another faith wanted to have a prayer group?"

I said, "In general, from what I understand about the law, you would need to try to provide a place for them to pray. And that would apply to any group who desires to pray."

The concern that other faiths may want to have a prayer group *should not,* in my opinion, be the reason you do not have them.

We've got to get over this phobia of integrating our faith with our work. God made us to be whole people, not people who live one way at home with our faith and another way at work, all stoic and, well, seemingly faithless. I guarantee you'll be surprised at the reactions of people who see how things like purpose, values, and prayer impact a work environment.

WORK IT OUT

It's not enough to simply write down some good-sounding words and call that your values list. You must put some thought into it. Here are a few thoughts to keep in mind as you build your list of values.

1. Why do you want *that* particular value, and how will it play out in real time?

2. Don't write values that you don't intend on applying to yourself personally. Remember, culture falls. These must begin in your own life. They must influence how you live at home and in the community. It's only a matter of time before someone discovers, "Hey, this guy preaches this at work, but have you seen him at his son's baseball games?"

3. Think about the values you most treasure. One of my good buddies treasures the value of honor. It's a big deal to him, and I see that in his life. He loves to honor people. So, it makes sense for him to list honor as one of his defining values. Be yourself.

....

CHAPTER 5

REIGNITE THE PASSION FOR GROWTH

If God was the owner, I was the manager. I needed to adopt a steward's mentality toward the assets He had entrusted—not given—to me. A steward manages assets for the owner's benefit. The steward carries no sense of entitlement to the assets he manages. It's his job to find out what the owner wants done with his assets, then carry out his will.

—Randy Alcorn

His master replied, "Well done, good and faithful servant! You have been faithful with a few things; I will put you in charge of many things. Come and share in your master's happiness!"

—Matthew 25:23, NIV

Great freedom awaits the leader who can view assets and resources as gifts to be stewarded rather than objects to be owned or held. Stewardship is about driving and managing growth.

So often, the idea of stewardship gets relegated to simple asset management. But I want to renew the concept of stewardship and give a more complete view of the idea. A stewardship perspective allowed our company to make a positive impact in the community and beyond through serving and quiet giving.

When we adopted a stewardship mentality, it ignited our passion for our community, rejuvenated our care for one another, and made everyone excited about growth. Over the next two chapters I want to dive into this idea of stewardship and how it can radically transform the way you view your company and its resources. One of my aha moments was understanding how stewardship and growth connect.

TWO AVENUES OF GROWTH

Stewardship requires you to view growth as an essential part of your life and business. We perform at our best when we are healthy and strong in all areas of our life. Your ideas, your talents and gifts, and all the things God's given to you are diminished when you're not healthy, if you're not vibrant and ready to take life on full steam ahead.

Earlier I talked about being a steward of everything God had given to me. It was my wake-up call when I realized that I'm accountable for all these gifts I've been given. I mean that personally and professionally. But how can I steward anything if I don't take care of myself?

Mental, spiritual, and physical growth is a must for any person who wants to stay healthy and strong. So it is with business. In light of these truths, I believe we need to reignite our passion for growth as a way to steward what we've been given. When we do, it's easy to see how the cycle works.

First, you must grow people. They are the heart and soul of any company.

Second, as a company, you must maintain a mentality that sees growth as a proactive way to stay healthy, solvent, and profitable.

The result? If you are not a healthy growing company, then you can't steward your resources because you'll be too busy trying to stay afloat. Let's look at a couple of ways we try to keep growing as individuals at our company.

GROW YOUR PEOPLE

One way we grow as individuals at Coca-Cola Consolidated is by taking part in mentoring programs. Like most organizations, we have many different growth and development programs for our people. We must continually grow and develop our teammates. The programs I've seen have the greatest impact are our mentor programs. These programs are based on the process developed by Regi Campbell called Radical Mentoring (www.RadicalMentoring.com) and the Known Collective (knownandworthy.com).

Radical Mentoring takes all the guesswork out of mentoring. In fact, they take care of all the work and preparation for you. You pick the mentoring topic and the training material from their website. It was so easy to use that I could no longer offer the excuse that there was too much prep work required to be a good mentor. It is all there for you—books, details, instructions, articles on all the topics like marriage, prayer, purpose, leadership, temptation, and servant leadership, among others. You name the topic and the resources, and this website provides everything else for you. It's a brilliant resource and no-nonsense way to incorporate mentoring into your personal life and into your organization's culture.

This program suggests you meet together monthly for twelve months. In addition to these monthly meetings, we do two weekend retreats during the year. But it's more than meetings and the retreats. In between the meetings each person in the group works through a book study. It's a little bit like having homework, but the good kind that you can't wait to sink your teeth into.

We also give a short assignment that's a simple one-page reflection on what we've learned during that month. I don't know if you've ever been part of a group like this, but I tell you what, it's great getting back together knowing that we're not going to just sit there like bumps on a log and wonder what we should talk about. We've done the reading and collected our thoughts, and we discuss.

And we're never at a loss of topics to discuss. One of the reasons I love this program so much is because we talk about relevant issues that pertain to our lives right here and now. Every topic you can think of as it relates to your vocational life, your family life, and beyond, we discuss. Put the vast array of topics with the routine reading and reflections, and you have the making for a dynamic time of growth. And I believe that's why the program is successful, especially for us at Coca-Cola Consolidated; people want this in their lives. They want to talk with their colleagues who've been there and done that and with others who are struggling through life right along with them. We grow better as human beings when we stay together, talk with one another, and pray for each other. And that's what this program does.

It's a serious program, and we love it. The magic number in the class is eight. It's eight because Regi said so. He was the pro at mentoring! Jesus had twelve, but he was Jesus.

We started mentoring our leaders eight years ago, and the growth of these mentor groups is now beginning to take off. Each person mentored agrees that down the road they will take what they have learned and start another mentor group of eight. Think about how the impact of mentoring multiplies over time. It's a staggering thought. I'm not a mathematician, but let's look at the numbers:

I start with a group of eight participants.

Then each of those eight also start a group in the following three to five years.

That's eight groups of eight—suddenly, we're at sixty-four leaders mentored.

Then each of those sixty-four leaders start a group of eight—now we're at 512 new leaders mentored.

Each of those 512 starts a group of eight, and we're at 4,096 leaders.

Over the next decade, hundreds and even thousands of our

leaders will be impacted through mentoring. The person who commits to the yearlong mentor program graduates a changed person; they leave a better mom, wife, husband, dad, son, daughter—a better and stronger leader. They understand the power of servant leadership, how to manage money, and how to become a giver. (We'll get more into the art of giving in a bit.)

Our president, Dave Katz, introduced these mentoring programs to our company, and together we have served as mentor leaders for many years now. To date, the two of us have mentored sixty-four leaders. And remember, they, in turn, will mentor eight groups, so eventually 512 leaders will be mentored, and their lives will be changed for good, for God, and for growth.

And by the way, Dave and I are getting so much from these annual mentoring sessions I can't envision we will ever stop. The day you or your organization stops growing, you've got to step in and revive yourself, your people, and the company.

I love seeing the year-end growth most of all. And I mean that for myself as well. When we start the program, understandably some participants are tentative. But by the end of the year, men and women who never prayed with their children are sharing how they spend time in prayer with their families. They understand the importance of giving the time, resources, and money to God and putting it to work for his kingdom. They grasp the very real spiritual battles that happen in the world. By the end of the year, men and women see the importance of cultivating a spiritual life.

I can't stress enough the power of mentoring. Think about this fact: Jesus spent three years mentoring the men and women who followed him. Of all those who followed him, he focused on twelve men. Of those twelve, three were his closest friends: Peter, James, and John. Mentorship lies at the heart of growth. When we commit to each other, so to speak, we invite accountability, and we encourage each other toward wholehearted transformation. And these are keys to growing as a person. When we shut people out, and we don't open ourselves up to someone who is wiser, we rob ourselves and others of the wonderful gifts that come with helping others sift through this journey of life.

CULTIVATE STRONG RELATIONSHIPS OUTSIDE OF WORK

My growth is all about my relationship with Christ. As a Christian, it's important to maintain a flourishing relationship with Jesus Christ. You do this the same way you would with any relationship. However, instead of talking to another person like yourself, you spend time in daily prayer and Bible study talking to God.

When my relationship with the Lord is strong, then I'm strong and growing. When I'm weak here, I'm not much of a leader, husband, or father. I've got to be disciplined about my daily time reading and studying God's Word (the Bible). I consider it the guide or manual for my life. When I make it the most important thing, life, business, and family go well.

That's not the sole reason why I do it; it's simply one of the by-products of cultivating a close relationship with God. I pursue Jesus because I love him and want to follow him and believe that by doing so I enrich my life and others' for good. It's the same with your relationships with friends and family. When they're healthy, life feels more joyful, less stressful. You might still encounter bumps in the road, but when your relationships are good and thriving, then it feels easier to get through hard times. That's what I mean when I say that when my relationship with Jesus is going well, other things seem to fall in place. I'm describing the joy that comes from knowing and following Christ, and that joy transcends the hardships life throws at you.

"What does your day look like pursuing a relationship with Jesus, Frank?" you ask.

"Well, that's a great question. I'll explain."

I start my day with time in the Bible and praying. It's so important to get wisdom and direction and to ask God for help and guidance as your day begins. I pray for wisdom every day. As you know, there are so many decisions we have to make where we have all the "facts" but have no idea what to do. That's where wisdom comes in, and wisdom comes from God. We've got to pray and ask God for the answers. He has them, because he himself *is* wisdom. The Bible says, "If any of you lacks wisdom, you should ask God, who gives generously to all without finding fault, and it will be given him" (James 1:5, NIV). You see, wisdom is there for the asking. I don't know about you, but I ask *a lot*.

KEEP YOU AND YOUR PEOPLE HEALTHY

I've touched a bit on personal and spiritual health, but I also want to encourage you to stay *physically* healthy. It's an invaluable part of the growth plan. Since graduating from college, exercise has been an important commitment for me, and I now exercise about five days a week and try to eat healthy.

"Eat your vegetables, Frank!"

"Of course!"

It's never too late to get on a program or workout regimen that makes sense for you. Decide today you are going to eat right and exercise at least three days a week. We want you around for the long term. You want to finish life strong, and you can do that.

"But, Frank, what do you mean by 'eat right'?"

"Good question!"

Listen, I'm no health expert, but I've found that simple tweaks to my diet impact my energy, productivity, and mood. I'm not saying you have to follow my example, but just having a plan in place that helps you stick to a healthy diet can do wonders for your peace of mind—and your gut.

Dr. Richard Furman, the co-founder of World Medical Mission, the medical arm of Samaritan's Purse, wrote a book called *Prescription for Life: Three Simple Strategies to Live Younger and Longer*. He'd be the first to tell you, the three strategies are not life-shattering epiphanies. In fact, you probably already know them. But like so many things in life, it's a matter of committing to them. They are

1. Exercise

2. Monitor your ideal weight

3. Eat a healthy diet

Nothing special, right? But Dr. Furman reminds us that we reap what we sow. A lifestyle of eating junk food, or sitting around, and carrying a few extra pounds will catch up with us one day or another. Every day we wake, we have the opportunity to sow some new seeds.

He suggests aiming for first achieving your ideal weight. Do what you need to do to reach that goal. If you need to try intermittent fasting, then do it. If you need to cut out sweets and eating after supper, then do both.

Once you reach your ideal weight, promise yourself that you're never going to leave that weight. And how will you do that? Exercise! The number one muscle in your body is your heart. And how do you keep it healthy? Moving your body with rigorous exercise. He says the key to having the strongest possible heart is maintaining a lifestyle of exercise.

Finally, he affirms what we touched on previously, and that is what you eat is of utmost importance. He tells the story of how he'd reached his ideal weight but was still eating foods that would clog his arteries, thus weakening his heart. When he read about the harmful effects of dietary cholesterol and saturated fats, he was all in on developing these three key areas to healthy living.

It's not that he wanted to stop the aging process. He makes the fascinating point that after the age of forty, what matters most is how old you are physiologically. That's right. You might be fifty-five, but your physiological age might be close to seventy. That's not good. He made it his goal to die young but at an old age. What he means by that is he wants to die physiologically younger than his age. What a great perspective and what an inspiration for healthy living.[6]

I've always understood the importance of growth in our business. But today, I understand it at a deeper level. It's more than just growing the bottom line. Growth that lasts is holistic growth that involves pursuing God; that pursuit results in a person who grows spiritually. And when we realize that we are God's workmanship and that he made us so that we might glorify him with our lives, then it's easy to understand the importance of healthy living as well.

I'll never forget a growth conversation I had with a friend of mine a few years ago. He and his family own a number of restaurant franchises, and I asked him how his business was doing. He responded by saying his business was "flat to down, but in this day and time, I guess that's okay." I can still remember challenging him that his view wasn't good. When things start to flatten out, we get very concerned and try to figure out how to get growth back into the equation. I might add that since our conversation, my friend's business has begun to grow again, and he even began acquiring new franchises.

Growth is not only good, it is godly; it's the right thing to do. We must stay focused on growth. The growth culture has to go down deep within your organization.

GROWTH REQUIRES INTENTIONALITY

On the corporate side, growth is vital to any company, and you must fight to keep it that way. After all, you can't steward resources if your company is not healthy.

On the company side of things, we believe our organization should be growing in every area of the business. Our financial results should be steadily improving. When our key growth numbers flatten out, we get nervous and upset. Growth is a mandate—not in a legalistic way but in the same vein as if you planted something like a garden. If you didn't see growth, you'd wonder, "Man, what's going on here? Why aren't my cucumbers growing?" Our businesses should be growing.

If business is flattening out, you immediately begin to ask the same questions as the gardener: What are the problems? How do we address the issues? How do we get the growth back?

I remember the 2008–9 recession quite well. Our company results started to flatten, and a flatlining business leads to the business cemetery, if you know what I mean.

So, what did we do? When things get tight, it's time to reevaluate. We tried to ask the *right* questions: What are the issues here? Where can we find the growth we need? What are we good at? What else should we be doing? It was time to move and take action. Our thinking had to change; we had to be open to doing things differently. And we did.

First of all, we took a hard look at our business and evaluated where we were growing and where we were stagnant. And we asked ourselves, Where is the business *going*?

Here's my point: When your business starts to flatten out—and when your culture starts to flatten out too—you need to move. Transformation is required. Growth is vital to the health of any company, and sometimes you have to do a little moving and shaking of your own to remain healthy, strong, and growing. I can assure you it will take courage; it will take new and fresh and, oftentimes, very uncomfortable, nontraditional ways of looking at how you do things and why. They say that it's always best to stay in your swim lane. I say, every once and a while, find a new swim lane to gain a fresh perspective. When is the last time you did that?

THANK GOD FOR THE 2008 RECESSION ERA

Isn't it interesting how difficult times lead to growth? Hard times wake you up and cause you to think outside the box and make changes.

A first simple step in being a growth company is to cultivate a growth mindset. You have to think of growth as a requirement, a mandate. Your company culture must be about growth. And remember, I'm not emphasizing the bottom-line growth first. The trick is to continue to grow our people. As I said earlier, companies do not grow. Our people grow, then the company grows. When this mindset takes hold, your team members will naturally think about growth as normal, and tough times as opportunities rather than setbacks. That's a recipe for innovation and success.

As an example of a wake-up call, during the same '08 recession, we had to reexamine everything we were doing and innovate again. As we were thinking outside of the hundred-year Coca-Cola Consolidated box, we began to ask ourselves what other businesses we were in or could be in that would strengthen our core business, the Coca-Cola business. We soon realized we were in the transportation business. We were shipping our beverages all over the Southeast from manufacturing centers to distribution centers.

We were also delivering hundreds of tractor trailer loads of our products to customers such as Walmart, Kroger, and Food Lion. We began to think seriously about being in the transportation business. About a year later we were there, and our first customers were some of our suppliers and other Coke bottlers and retail customers.

The Coke name for quality and service was powerful. We began to rapidly pick up new customers. As a new entrant in the transportation business, our company, now called Red Classic Services, was on the move and growing. The company officially started in 2010. Over the past five years we have been growing the business at a healthy rate year over year. Wow! Thank God for the recession.

With a growth mindset, you begin to see hard times and negatives as opportunities to change things up. But the real key is to think this way in good times. Take action and move into new territory when things are going well.

ONE-ON-ONE

We live in a world that has a hard time committing to, well, anything. We like to keep our options open, because there's so much to choose from. If you don't like something you purchased at the store, return it—or just throw it out and buy something else. It's a mundane example of commitment, but it's true, nonetheless. Some say it's because our culture is so transient. We don't keep jobs for more than three to five years now. We'll not only switch jobs, but we'll also hopscotch careers. Finding a skilled craftsman has become increasingly rare. Craftsmanship takes commitment, and that's just something that has gone by the wayside in our society. I know what you're thinking. How does commitment relate to growth?

Think about a company in which employees turn over every three to five years. First, that's hard on the culture. It breeds unrest and uncertainty. And who wants that? When leadership doesn't commit to team members, team members will, in turn, give up on the leadership.

But when leadership shows commitment to their vision and team members by committing to a growth culture, that says something to everyone. It says, "Hey, we are here for the long haul. We believe that if we stick together and focus and commit to our vision, then we will see great gains, both as a company and as individuals." One of the most important business principles to achieving long-term success is long-term commitment to the business.

But what does long-term success look like? Now, that's a rabbit trail I can't resist.

Before we answer that, we need to establish a working definition for success. Some might say, "Isn't success when you make a lot of money, you have several houses, and you own lots of cars and toys?" No, not really. That is more excess than success. But I can see why some would say that. In our world, we too often associate the monetary or material results that come when we win at our work. But, as a Christian, I believe true success involves much more than toys and mounds of cash.

I believe true success is knowing God's will and purpose for your life, for your company, and then going out and fulfilling that purpose. When I'm accomplishing my purpose, that's when I know I am achieving true success. See, I told you *purpose* was important!

I hear so many leaders talk about vision, and I love talking about it too. But I believe the greatest vision we can have for ourselves and our companies comes through discovering God's will for our lives and companies, and then going out there and doing it. Pursuing our God-given purpose leads to accomplishing our vision, which results in true success.

Committing to growth says something about your leadership to those whom you seek to serve. It tells them you're in it for the long haul, for the betterment of everyone. This kind of commitment breeds long-term success—a success that looks like a company fulfilling its purpose.

WORK IT OUT

When your business begins to show signs of stagnation, it's time to shake things up. Purpose-driven individuals and companies constantly pursue growth. Growth is a sign of life. It signals vibrancy, health, and fun. What are some basic things you can do to cultivate a growth mentality? Here are five for you to tuck into your field bag (or whatever kind of bag suits your fancy).

1. **Reevaluate**: When downtimes come, view them as opportunities to hold everything up to the light. What's working? What's not? What falls in line with your purpose? What's crept in that's stealing precious energy from achieving your goals?

2. **Be open to change**: Don't let sameness steal your creative juices. Sure, you've done such-and-such program forever. All programs run their course. Change

will invigorate you and your leaders. Change will create excitement for your team members, too.

3. **Be honest about what's failing**: Be real with yourself and know when it's time for a change. This requires a no-nonsense view of your company's effectiveness. No sacred cows!

4. **Take action**: Don't fall asleep at the wheel. Growth doesn't just happen. It demands action. You must tend to your business like a gardener to the soil. Roll up your sleeves and get your hands dirty. Get involved. Get busy. Grow big.

5. **Embrace risk**: There's no such thing as safe in the business world. You must get comfortable with taking a chance on an outlier idea. Chaplaincy, for us, was an outlier idea. But we didn't shy away from it. We went for it. And not a day goes by that I'm not thankful we took that risk.

J. B. Harrison, Greensboro, NC   1st Coke Franchise, 1902

Original Coca-Cola bottling facility in Charlotte

Frank and his father. Left to right: Frank Harrison, Jr., Frank Harrison

A visit with Dr. Billy Graham.
Left to right: Frank Harrison, Dr. Billy Graham, Frank Harrison, Jr.

Frank enjoying a Coke with Simon and Sosthen—the first Mobile Messengers.
Left to right: Simon K., Frank Harrison, Sosthen A.

Open Eyes' first vision trip to India

Kamal—our first visit with Kamal in Sudan

Pastor training in Kenya. Open Eyes Mobile Messengers

Open Eyes' Sudanese leadership. Mobile Messengers from Sudan

James in Lui, Sudan, 2006

James in Lui, Sudan, 2006

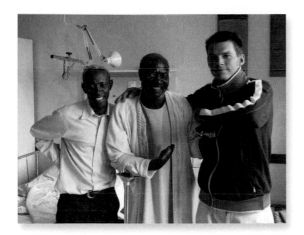

James and Simon visiting
Kamal in the hospital.
Left to right: Simon K.,
Kamal, James Harrison

Peter Freissle receiving the Bob Pettus
Great Commission Award at t-factor in
April 2015. Left to right: Bob Pettus, Peter
Freissle, Matthew Freissle, Frank Harrsion.
Photography by Ingrid Wilson Narratives.

Coca-Cola Consolidated Response Team serving in
Wilmington, NC, after Hurricane Florence. Left to right:
Brian Nick, Frank Harrison, Emilie Nichols

Frank addressing leaders during t-factor in Washington, DC

....

CHAPTER 6

UNDERSTAND THE POWER OF GENEROSITY

*You have not lived today until you have done something for
someone who can never repay you.*

—John Bunyan

What is the power of a gift? What happens when
a true gift is given? When someone experiences
true generosity?

So much is made of the person or company that gives in a
public fashion. But giving is about so much more than a mention in the media.

The true giver does not give to receive accolades. Instead, she gives out of a sense of personal responsibility and genuine love for her community and for her fellow man. She gives to help and inspire. Transformational leaders transform cultures by embracing a posture of generosity—in giving of both time and resources.

Let's take what we've learned about stewardship and cultivating a growth mentality a step further and explore what it means to adopt a lifestyle of generosity that extends beyond the giving of money. I believe that such a lifestyle communicates the truth that when you do good for the community from a pure and honest place, the community will support you, which in turn, feeds growth.

KNEELING TO LEAD

A couple of years ago, I was visiting one of our production centers in Sandston, Virginia. We had recently acquired the Coke franchise, and I was sharing with the leadership team about our business and mentioned the concept of servant leadership. One of our supervisors on the front row said she had never heard of servant leadership.

I remember thinking, *This concept will totally revitalize her leadership when she begins to understand the power of serving others.*

I remember moving toward her and saying, "I don't know what you think or know about Jesus Christ, but he was a great leader who lived two thousand years ago. His organization is still thriving with billions of professing followers around the world today. And here's how he led."

I told her the story about how Jesus washed the feet of his disciples right before he was taken by the temple guard and accused of blasphemy.

When all the disciples were together for the feast of Passover, a long-held Jewish tradition, he stood up from his place at the table, and with a towel around his waist and a bowl of water in his hands, he began to wash their feet. The custom back then was that the lowest servant would wash the guests' feet. For example, let's say I stopped by your house for a visit, and we lived in Jesus's hometown of Nazareth. It would be customary for you to have your servant greet me by washing my feet. Then we'd continue on into your house and visit and probably eat some good food.

Jesus's act was radical in his culture. Rabbis, what we would call a teacher, did not take off their outer garments and kneel down and wash the feet of their followers, and Jesus was considered to be a teacher, a rabbi. When Jesus stooped down and began to wash his disciples' feet, it would have caused them great alarm. It was completely countercultural.

In the story, which you can find in the Bible (John 13:1–17, NIV), Peter, one of Jesus's closest friends and a leader among his disciples, reacted with indignation. "You will never wash my feet," he said to Jesus.

"If I do not wash your feet, you will have no part with me," Jesus said.

Peter relented and allowed Jesus to wash his feet.

Can you imagine the scene? Jesus used this radical act to show his disciples how they were to serve one another after he was gone. When he had finished washing their feet, he told them to do likewise.

A LEADER OF UNEXPECTED KINDNESS

Jesus taught his disciples that the greatest among them would be the servant of all (Matthew 23:11–12, NIV). Remember, *serving others* is one of the five characteristics of the transformational leader—leaders who understand they were not appointed to be served but to serve others. And the foot-washing act was his example to them of this very principle. Jesus taught them that the way up in life is to go down.

After I told her the story, I went down on my knees as if I was going to wash her feet. She seemed emotionally moved as I was explaining the concept of serving at the lowest level. It's an act that forces both parties involved to really think about how we need to serve one another.

The principle of generosity carries more meaning than simply giving someone or a cause a lot of money. You do not have to be rich to be generous. Some are unable to give money, but they are generous in other ways. Generosity also entails sharing unexpected kindness and blessing others. When I think of the heart of a generous person, I think of Jesus. He was the Son of God, and yet he gave freely of himself. Washing his disciples' feet was an act of kindness and love.

After he washed their feet, he went to the cross and died for the sins of all mankind. The generous spirit gives until it hurts. The generous spirit does not follow expected social norms but finds ways to subvert the culture with the blessing of love and service.

For us, I think it should be far easier to be generous when it comes to our monetary giving.

"Well, what makes you say that, Frank?"

"Oh, I'm glad you asked!"

Because it's not ours to begin with! We're stewards! And our master is the most generous master a servant could want. Generosity, for us, should come from a stewardship mentality. It's not our own; it's been given to us so that we might use it for God's glory and serve our fellow man. See, there's that purpose statement again. Giving generously falls right in line with our purpose. So, we embrace it and do it freely and joyfully, excited to see what God does with it.

GO AHEAD, TEST GOD

I know generosity in a world that is often self-centered and preoccupied with wealth and power can seem countercultural or stretch our thinking, but stay with me. I think it feels that way because we've been ingrained with the idea that power is money and money is influence, and we should get as much of it as we can. But a transformational leader sees generosity differently. She understands the power and amazing things that happen when we practice generosity in our giving.

There are many verses that address the subject of giving. I love the verse Malachi 3:10 (NIV). It says (short version): "Give, I will bless you, test me, says the Lord."

I understand this verse to be the only time in the Bible where God says, "Test me." Isn't it interesting that it's around the subject of giving? God is so confident you will be blessed, he says, "Test me. Go ahead and give, and watch the blessings come." The longer version of that verse says, "Give and I will throw open the gates of heaven and pour out so much blessing you will not be able to store it."

You know that old slogan "You can't out-give God"? Well, it's true.

Once, I was in an accountability conversation with one of our business leaders about our giving, and he pointed out to me that our giving at Coca-Cola Consolidated had exceeded our budget. We never like to exceed an expense budget, but sometimes on the giving side we may encounter a special opportunity to significantly impact the lives of people for the long term. When that happens, and we have the resources to do so, it's our great pleasure to make a special gift.

I agreed with the fact we had exceeded the giving budget in the past year, but added the company performed very well over that same period of time. I pointed out, "We actually more than doubled the size and market value of the company over the past three-year period."

He, of course, realized the company had dramatically grown during the past few years, and he agreed with me that things were going well financially. What a humbling realization to discover that, indeed, God's Word is true and trustworthy. What a blessing it was to look back over those three years and see the faithfulness of God in our growth. I'm convinced godly growth comes in part from acts of generosity.

We give because it's the right thing to do. And we never run out of opportunities to give because there are so many needs right here at home, not to mention those around the world. But it is a fact that God pours out his blessings when we give. I've never read it in a business book, but over the past 25 years, I've seen how generosity drives cash flow. Like it or not, we are known in our community as givers or takers—be a giver. In general, at the end of it all, givers win and takers lose. The Bible actually speaks to this principle: Proverbs 11:24–25 (MSG) says, "The world of the generous gets larger and larger; the world of the stingy gets smaller and smaller. The one who blesses others is abundantly blessed; those who help others are helped."

ONE-ON-ONE

Earlier I talked about the mentoring program, but I want to come back to the topic again and offer you some personal encouragement. I remain an active mentor as part of my own effort to grow personally. I am now in my eighth year of mentoring a group of eight throughout the year. By the time the year is over, we've discussed all the important areas of life, such as marriage, money, leadership, temptation, the Bible, prayer, and purpose. The list goes on and on.

We all experience deep impact from the year's worth of meetings. I delight in seeing how everyone grows in wisdom and godliness—including myself! The program shapes us into godly leaders for the home and the marketplace. The transformation is remarkable.

One of the key topics every year is money and what you do with it. Do you spend it, invest it, or give it away? Most of us have never been taught principles of biblical stewardship and giving, so this point in our mentoring provides a great opportunity for our mentees to enter into a dialogue on the topic.

The typical answer to "How much do you give away each year?" is "If I have some money left over at the end of the year, we give to various charities." Many people have no clear direction or understanding of what God's Word says about giving but are enthusiastic about learning more. They don't understand the joy of giving and the blessings that go along with it, but they soon start to understand and enter into the joy giving can bring.

I've also discovered over the years that companies and other organizations—for profit and nonprofit—don't really fully understand giving either. For example, how much should an individual or a corporation give away each year? And who should they give it to?

By now, I hope you understand these "One-on-One" sections as a time where we get more personal, as if we were sitting and enjoying a Coke together. For this one, I actually want to set up the "Work It Out" section that follows by encouraging you in two ways.

First, don't put off giving until you have loads of money. Giving is not about the amount of money you have and can give. It's about the posture of your heart. God just wants you to be a giver—he doesn't care if you're a millionaire or a college student. Give out of the bounty he's given you to steward.

Second, God loves a cheerful giver. Give from the joy in your heart. Forget about the blessing part of it; give because of the joy you get when you help someone through generosity.

Okay, now with our hearts ready to give, let's look at how we can work this out in our lives and businesses.

WORK IT OUT

Let's talk about how much of your hard-earned money you should give away. Individuals *and* corporations should give generously to causes and charities they believe in and that support the communities where they live and work.

How Much Should You Give?

Without going through all the verses in the Bible on giving, I would summarize and say that ten percent of your income, what is known as a tithe, is the amount God asks us to give in his Word. That one is hard to argue with.

As an individual, I believe the tithe (ten percent) should be given *plus* an offering. I was taught this as a child growing up, so it has always been easy for me to be a tither. When we got our allowance as kids, we knew that ten percent was coming out of it and going to God's work. I've noticed with others who didn't have this training, like some of the members in my mentor group, it's difficult to give the tithe. I encourage them to start at two percent and work up to ten percent.

I realize the concept of giving to God can be difficult to grasp for some people, especially if they didn't have the type of upbringing I did. For me, it became second nature. I was blessed. Here's what I tell people who struggle with giving to God: You've got to realize that God owns it all.

Sometimes, I think, *Okay, this is really God's money; now how much of his money should I give back to him?*

Right now, if God gives me ten dollars, I have grown

beyond the giving of my one-dollar tithe and into deeper and deeper levels of generosity in its many forms. But listen, that's me. Remember, God wants a cheerful giver. It's important to understand that giving isn't just something that you *do*. It's an *attitude* you cultivate. It needs to come from your heart.

My advice? Give ten percent a try and see what regular giving does to your heart. Experience the joy that comes in seeing God use your money for his good purposes. I've a hunch that when you experience the joy of giving, you'll get hooked and want to give more, and in different ways and to different groups and organizations.

And remember, one of these days our time here on earth will be over. Our possessions here on earth will not matter. Here's a newsflash: We can't take any money with us when we die. What will become of my money when I'm gone? Will it be sitting in some bank account somewhere doing nothing? Or will it be invested in the future?

The Bible says store up for yourselves treasure in heaven, not on earth. I want to invest in the *future*. Let's be eternal investors. I promise, you will never regret it.

How Much Should Your Business Give?

Now what about your business? Should you give? How much and to whom? And on the how much, what percent of that should you give to whom? Wow, that's a lot of questions.

Let me begin by saying I believe it is important for your corporation to give. It is absolutely good for business. As we discussed earlier, giving leads to growth. And, like it or not, you and your company will either be known as a giving organization or as, well, stingy. People will either say, "They are so generous" or "They never give anything to anyone." Which company do you prefer to do business with? A generous one, or a stingy one? Which company are you? I know, these are hard questions. But good, nonetheless.

Our research on this topic revealed most companies give about one to two percent of pretax income, and they feel very good about that. Other companies use the tithing principle and give ten percent. And then there are companies like Hobby Lobby who give fifty percent of their pretax income to charitable causes.

At times, a legacy of giving is passed down from one generation to another, but in our experience most companies do not consider giving in a systematic way. Our company didn't give much to charitable causes in our earlier days. But about twenty years ago we woke up to the power and joy of giving. We gave to the normal things—education, the arts and sciences, the poor—but we really never considered faith-based organizations that support our communities as part of our overall giving strategy or portfolio.

We let that kind of giving go until we received the wake-up call around stewardship and the realization that someday we would be held accountable for our giving. We woke up and began to assess and increase our overall giving strategy. We broke our giving into three buckets—body, mind, and spirit. We became focused on meeting physical, emotional, and spiritual needs through our charitable giving.

At present, our giving philosophy has moved beyond the

one to two percent of pretax giving benchmark mentioned earlier as we continue to recognize the deep needs in so many communities. We have a growing awareness of people struggling all around us—homelessness, addiction, people with too little to eat, illiteracy, elder care, widow care, orphan care, prison ministries, education, the arts, health service—all kinds of opportunities for giving.

If you have to ask the question, "To whom do we give as an organization?" then you're not looking hard enough. So many other organizations in this great nation work tirelessly to meet the desperate needs of our cities and communities. Just take some time, put in some due diligence, research some of your favorite organizations, and give.

There is no shortage of wonderful causes to invest in. The challenge, of course, is to figure out where your calling is, where you should invest, and how much your investment should be. On where to invest, we began to do the research on the needs of different communities. Then we could make an informed decision as to where we were going to give. As you discover the needs and pray about them, you will begin to feel a calling in certain directions.

A Few Tips on Creating Giving Funds

Regional market unit funds: We have several different giving funds at Coca-Cola Consolidated. Our Coke territories span fourteen states and the District of Columbia and are divided into several market units. We give each market unit funds to give in their area. We give general guidelines as to how these dollars should be given, but our local market unit vice presidents know and seek to address the needs in their communities.

Corporate funds: We have a line item in our budget for our annual giving, and a contribution committee helps direct that giving. We focus on mind, body, and spirit giving. We get many requests and sometimes do our own projects. Each request is considered and prayed over, and then a giving decision is made.

Long-term sustained giving funds: We also established separate charitable giving funds years ago and contribute to these funds every year to enable us to continue giving generously in lean business years.

Your Challenge

Test out the verse Malachi 3:10 by being a generous giver, and see what happens. Try to out-give God.

I promise you; he will bless you as he promised. You will never regret being a generous giver. Remember, "Whoever sows sparingly will also reap sparingly, and whoever sows generously will also reap generously."

CHAPTER 7

....

LEAD COURAGEOUSLY

*You must never be fearful about what you
are doing when it is right.*

—Rosa Parks

*Courage is not the absence of fear, but the triumph over it.
The brave man is not he who does not feel afraid,
but he who conquers that fear.*

—Nelson Mandela

You must kneel to lead.

That is where the generous spirit of the leader is forged. In the last chapter, I used the example of Jesus washing his disciples' feet as a way to show you the posture of a transformational leader. I want to come back to it for a moment and tell you about my first time washing someone's feet.

If you've never washed someone's feet, I would encourage you to do it. I'll never forget the first feet I washed. It was about ten years ago. I was in our kitchen with my son, James, and my wife, Jan. James was getting ready to return to Africa to continue his humanitarian and missions work.

We were talking about the ministry Samaritan's Feet and how they wash people's feet, give them a new pair of shoes, and share the message of Christ with them.

"James," I said, "I want to wash your feet."

"Sure, Dad," he said. "Go right ahead."

I got a bucket and filled it with warm water in the kitchen sink. Then I walked over to James, who was sitting in a chair, and got down on my knees. As I was putting his feet into the bucket of warm water, I looked up at him, and he looked down at me, and we both began to tear up. It was a powerful, moving moment. The first feet I ever washed were the feet of my son, James.

What a great picture of service Jesus gave to us. So many people want to be great leaders. And in our world, greatness and great leaders are associated with power and status. But Jesus showed us another way. We cannot lead courageously if we're not willing to humble ourselves, take a knee, and wash our neighbors' feet.

I believe Jesus was the greatest leader ever. No matter what you believe about Jesus, you can't deny his revolutionary approach to leadership. At Coca-Cola Consolidated we believe in a foot-washing kind of leadership: servant leadership. It's the core of the transformational leader; we believe we can all improve as servant leaders.

"But, Frank, I thought courageous leadership was more of a 'rah-rah, out in front, bringing attention to the self' kind of leadership."

I know it does seem like that should be the way of it. After all, our culture likes to paint the picture of the gallant warrior who faces the battle outnumbered and yet prevails in the battle. Of course, there is a courage appropriate for battle. I know it's popular to spin courage in the corporate context with a warrior kind of flair, barreling through enemy lines, unafraid of what's coming. The goal is to do whatever it takes to achieve the outcome we are chasing. But I'm here to tell you that if courage is the ability to do something that frightens you, then serving your fellow man is right up there. We don't like to serve others before ourselves. And though we say we may not be afraid of it, we certainly do not seek it out. Leading from the kneeling position feels vulnerable and weak, and the warrior must be strong and stand tall. Right?

Not quite. When I think of Jesus's example of washing his disciples' feet, I'm humbled to think that the God of the universe would come to earth as a carpenter and not only heal and serve his own creation but go on and die for them. Wow— that is mind-blowing. If leading by serving is good enough for God, well, it's more than good enough for me. And that's why I believe authentic, transformative, courageous leadership leads with knees bent, putting others first.

Don't get me wrong. I'm not up here on a pedestal preaching at you. I cannot help but share with you this great treasure I found after years of digging in the wrong field for it. As a company, we didn't always believe this way, but we've learned a few things over the years. When you truly serve—and I mean truly serve—your people, your customers, your family, and those around you, then they will follow you.

CARING IS COURAGEOUS

At Coca-Cola Consolidated we believe it's important to teach all of our teammates how to be servant leaders. A service-first mindset speaks volumes to customers. When we make it a priority and commit to serve our customers well, business will naturally grow. Let me give you an example.

There is a small convenience store in the town of Waxhaw right outside of Charlotte. I go by it on the way to our farm and stop there for a Coke and gas from time to time. The store owner is from South Korea, and his store was selling way too much of the blue stuff—you know what I mean. So I, along with our salespeople in that area, would work on him regularly to consider selling more of the red stuff, if you catch my meaning. But we were getting nowhere.

This struggle had gone on for a couple of years when I dropped in on him one Sunday afternoon. I'd been riding motorcycles with my son-in-law, Jay, and we were hot and thirsty. We sat down with him, enjoyed an ice-cold Coca-Cola, and began talking with him about his family.

We had chatted in the past, but our conversations were short and quick because I was always on the move. That day, for some reason, I decided to slow down and invest real quality time with him. I knew his son, who worked at the store, but I found out in our conversation that his daughter was facing much difficulty trying to immigrate to the United States. His story spoke to me, and I began to sympathize with his daughter's situation and offered to help her find a job here.

I could tell he was moved by my willingness to help, and I could tell he deeply missed his daughter. I never mentioned our

Coke business during the visit. I just listened and offered help when it seemed appropriate.

About a month later, I was driving by his store and couldn't believe my eyes. Outside of his store, all stacked up, was a ton of blue beverage equipment (you know, our competitor's). I pulled into the parking lot and walked into the store. It looked like a Coke museum in there. Coke equipment, coolers, and banners were everywhere. It was beautiful, and I immediately realized what had happened.

After three years of selling and asking for the business, I finally realized that I should just serve him and his family. When I stopped trying to sell myself and focused more on helping another person in their real-world situation, something miraculous happened. A bond of trust was created, and from that bond came the business.

Now, don't get me wrong. It's not a bait and switch. I'm just observing what naturally happens when you serve others. Something wonderful is created—a bond of trust. It doesn't always happen, nor is it the goal, but very often when you help someone first, good things ensue. In this case, the store owner's heart was touched, and he decided to be a Coke man. I loved it. I did not expect it, nor was I trying to be nice in order to get him to switch.

But this story also applies to business and how, when in a business context, serving plays such a vital role. S. Truett Cathy, the founder of Chick-fil-A, once said, "My business grew on my understanding that customers are always looking for somebody who is dependable and polite and will take care of them." At our deepest levels, we all want someone to care for us. Apply this to how you operate your business and your life, and incredible things happen.

EARNING TRUST IS COURAGEOUS

That's one simple story among hundreds. When our folks love and serve our customers at the deepest level, that's when business grows. In our age of over-the-top marketing and the always-on salesperson, we forget that business is all about the customer—meeting their needs and earning their trust.

It's easy to get caught up in the business of business—focusing on developing great brands, timely delivery, the right pricing and packaging strategies. It's also about meeting emotional, physical, and spiritual needs and loving and serving people.

I had the opportunity to spend some time with a former mayor of Baltimore, Maryland, and their staff. The mayor told me that at the time, one in ten of the residents of the city were heroin addicts. I remember thinking, *Wow, if Charlotte, North Carolina, has close to one million people, that means there would be one hundred thousand heroin addicts roaming the city.*

Through a recent acquisition of the Coke franchise in the region, our business led us to create a lasting presence in Baltimore. Upon hearing the mayor's story, I immediately realized we needed to get involved in an inner-city addiction ministry.

We heard about a wonderful ministry called Helping Up that was already doing good work in the city. We visited with their leaders and couldn't believe they had five hundred beds for addicts. They and their team loved, served, and discipled these people. Our Coke teammates got involved in feeding and serving also, and we made a solid financial investment in the ministry.

And we looked for more ways to make a possible contribution to the city by way of serving. We've worked with Samaritan's Feet in the past and have partnered with them in washing the feet of hundreds of kids from Baltimore and giving them new shoes while also sharing the love of Jesus with them. We wanted to serve this community, and as we did, we were able to get closer to the leaders, pastors, and community as a whole. As our opportunities to serve grew and spread, so did our opportunities to grow our business in the city.

Serving leads to growth. We serve because it is the right thing to do. As an added bonus, we get to see our company grow. It's a beautiful synergy, but it all begins with leaders who are courageous enough to bend their knees and care for others.

WE SERVE BECAUSE IT IS THE RIGHT THING TO DO

If there's one thing hurricanes are good for, it's giving us all opportunities to care for one another. When Hurricane Harvey hit Houston in August of 2017, a friend of mine emailed me and told me he was loading up a van with four or five guys and was going to Houston from Charlotte to help out. I got that email in the middle of the night, and I remember thinking, *What am I doing for those folks? What is Coca-Cola Consolidated doing?*

The answer was *Not a lot.* We may write a check to someone helping out, but I wondered if there wasn't more we could do.

The next day, I realized that there was more we could do, but we needed to learn how to do it. We called the folks at Samaritan's Purse, the experts at disaster relief and rapid response. They were kind enough to allow us to observe the wonderful work they were doing in Houston. From there, we began to assemble our first response team.

We purchased a trailer loaded with equipment, tools, power saws, whatever you would need in dealing with the aftermath of a hurricane, tornado, flood, or fire. We got the training. We were ready.

A few months later, Hurricane Florence crashed into the Wilmington, North Carolina, area and flooded homes, downed power lines, uprooted trees, and scattered branches. Our people living in the area were in trouble. We got the word out about our new response team, and the phone calls came in.

Our Coca-Cola Consolidated Response Team flew into action. Employee calls for help were answered as we deployed a team of volunteers to the affected homes.

I'll never forget one family whose house was covered with fallen trees and debris. The dad had gone to one of our Coke plants for work early in the morning. The response team arrived later in the morning. The team of ten went to work pulling trees off the house, clearing the yard, and gently moving power lines. About six hours later you couldn't believe the transformation.

The dad returned home after all the work was done, and he was floored when he saw what had been accomplished. His ten-year-old son said, "I can't believe my dad works for a company that would do this for us."

We also sent our chaplains along with the response team to serve and counsel our people.

There were many other stories as a result of Florence. Our Coke territory now runs up and down the East Coast, and I'm sure there will be more hurricanes, floods, and tornadoes. We want to be there for our people, because that's what families do for each other; we are family, and we serve each other.

Today we have several hundred volunteers for response, current and retired employees ready to serve during the next natural disaster. Our Coca-Cola Consolidated Response Team represents just one more way that you can serve people in your local community and beyond. But here's the bottom line: Serving requires only a willing heart and ready feet. Serving and caring for people in our own company and in our communities falls right in line with our purpose statement. If there's one thing that honors God, it's caring for his children. And that's what drives our efforts.

BUILD A COMPANY OF SERVANT LEADERS

If you want fired-up, motivated employees, give them the opportunity to serve. Our corporate culture transformation has produced people who love to serve, and their selflessness leads to uncommon growth.

If you ask me, one of the most fruitful seeds of transformation was our chaplaincy program. Once our chaplaincy program took off, our culture blossomed. We could feel the change but knew we needed to provide more opportunities for change. Our longtime human resources leader, the late Bob Pettus, told me that we needed to teach our employees how to become less selfish and more selfless; we needed to teach everyone the concept of servant leadership. We realized we needed to get our people out serving in the community.

That's why we started stewardship programs like our response team. Their goal? To meet physical, emotional, and spiritual needs for those whom we are serving. To date, we have cultivated and nurtured over one hundred steward-ship programs in our fourteen-state area and the District of Columbia. We work with and serve the homeless, orphans, prisoners, the elderly, and whoever our local operations want to serve in their communities.

Once you get courageous and begin leading by caring for the community, you'll find that God takes that action, those seeds sewn in good faith, and he harvests goodness.

Here's an example of what I mean. There is a deli sandwich shop near where I live called Phil's Deli. One day I walked in, and Phil began to tell everybody in the restaurant what a great company Coca-Cola Consolidated is in our community. I was a little confused at first, but then Phil told me that one of our stewardship teams had recently refurbished and repainted the Elon Homes and Schools for Children. This particular orphan-age was served by Phil and his people also. Our involvement with the orphanage had a significant impact on him. I was humbled by Phil's testimony and honored that he'd think so highly of our willingness to get into the community and serve those in need.

We were simply going about our business and trying to be consistent in our purpose as a company. God took that consistent contribution to the community and made it grow. Sometimes the smallest acts of kindness done with a pure heart and mind will reap a harvest you may never see. But it first requires us to step out, muster our courage, and do what's right for people in the community.

Remember, people who seek to lead courageously recognize and accept their responsibility to drive shareholder value for the organizations they lead, and recognize faithful stewardship mandates growth. Being a courageous leader begins with personal recognition of the greater purpose of their organization. Their recognition leads to a deeper understanding of their company's mission. They know that if the company does not grow well, then the company's mission will dim and even fail. And it is the creative ways in which they serve others that spur this growth, leading in a countercultural manner that will ignite others to roll up their sleeves and, well, wash someone's feet.

ONE-ON-ONE

Leading others gets lonely. I don't mean that in a lonesome sort of way. Instead, I mean you must be willing to stand alone with a decision, position, or action, or all of the above. Courageous leadership requires one to come to terms with his or her ability to turn right when everyone else is shouting, "No! Turn left!"

During those lonely times, a leader will find himself facing all kinds of obstacles: contrarians, naysayers, personal conflict, and heavy setbacks. But those come with the territory.

When I think about leaders facing difficult obstacles to overcome, the biblical story of Nehemiah comes to mind. Nehemiah was a Jew and former slave of the Persian Empire in 444 BC who fasted and prayed, and his life changed, and ultimately, he became the governor of Jerusalem.

His story goes like this: The nation of Israel had been living in Babylonian captivity for years. Their temple and home city were laid to waste. A small group of Jewish workers were sent back to Jerusalem seventy years before everyone else so that they could rebuild the temple. But Nehemiah discovered that the walls and gates of the city were destroyed and burned, and he wept.

Nehemiah felt a calling to return to Jerusalem and rebuild the walls. At that time, he was serving as the cupbearer for King Artaxerxes. One day, the king noticed Nehemiah looked sad, so he asked him what troubled him. Nehemiah spilled the beans and then asked his king to send him back so that he might rebuild the wall and gates of Jerusalem. The king agreed and sent Nehemiah back to his home city with supplies and gear and horses and even fighting men.

But some people who lived in the area of Jerusalem were not happy with Nehemiah's vision and purpose to rebuild the city wall and gates. They constantly mocked and jeered him and his working crew. Things got so bad that Nehemiah had to have some people work while others stood guard, fearing violent attacks.

Nehemiah faced all kinds of criticism. People made fun of him and laughed at him and threatened him with violence. But Nehemiah did not waver from his vision for rebuilding the wall of Jerusalem. According to the biblical account, Nehemiah rebuilt the wall of Jerusalem against seemingly impossible odds in just fifty-two days.

Three things stick out to me after reading Nehemiah's story.

First, he believed in and led with purpose. Purpose guides the way we serve and fuels our passion for the task at hand. We read in the book of Proverbs that "without vision the people perish." So true! Without vision and purpose, we drift through life and business rudderless.

Second, he faced big-time opposition and did not waver in his vision. This is so huge. It's easy to fold in the face of opposition. "Well, this must not be the right path or the right decision. God's not in this." That's a lie! Whoever said that God's blessings only rest on ventures that go smoothly? It's the difficult times that test our faith in God and grit to see a thing through.

Third, he persevered until the task was finished. I love Nehemiah's journey, because it began with him on his knees praying and fasting. His passion moved him, and his perseverance enabled him, through God's strength, to complete the task.

Leading courageously begins on our knees. It's a by-product of a heart given to God's purposes. But hardship will come. The courageous leader must refuse to respond with emotions to situations that, if escalated, could get dicey. Leaders have to show poise and restraint and a willingness to endure hardship even at the cost of their own comfort because they realize that in the end, it will be worth the effort, worth the hardship.

If you're out there leading today and this book has found its way into your hands, then I'm so happy to encourage you to stay the course. Don't give in! Get on your knees and transform the world, one prayer at a time.

WORK IT OUT

In his best-selling book *Good to Great*, author Jim Collins famously wrote, "Good is the enemy of great." That's one of the reasons few companies become great.

Later in the book, Collins wrote:

> "Those who turn good into great are motivated
> by a deep creative urge and an inner compul-
> sion for sheer unadulterated excellence for its
> own sake. Those who perpetuate mediocrity,
> in contrast, are motivated more by the fear
> of being left behind."[7]

Wow, do you see the contrast? Fear focuses our attention on the outward things, and we become ensnared in the pursuit of visible signs of success. But something deeper pulls on the leader who is motivated by significance rather than fear.

We desire that all our employees do their best, but not from a standpoint of fear of losing their job or any other kind of fear. We want their ambition to do their best to come from within. We want their work for our company to be an extension of their identity. And that, friends, comes from knowing your—let's say it together—purpose.

The courageous leader:

1. is motivated by significance rather than fear

2. fights for others in prayer

3. looks for ways to inspire others to serve with them

Your homework:

1. Write down your motivation for leading others.

2. Commit to praying for your team members and leaders.

3. Make a list of ideas that might inspire your team to serve better in the community.

HOW DID WE DO IT?

"But, Frank," you ask, "how have you applied courageous leadership with your team at Coca-Cola Consolidated?"

I figured you'd ask. So, what have we learned and how did we apply it to our community? Right. Let's dive in.

I can't emphasize this truth enough: When you get your culture right, it will drive your organization in the right direction. I believe most companies don't really know their culture. They have a mission statement, and some folks in the building might know it, but it doesn't permeate the organization. Remember, it's one thing to have your mission statement written on the company website, but it's quite another to work with living human beings who embody that mission day after day. That's where true transformation happens.

In the preceding chapters I tried to give you a good view of courageous steps we have taken to shape our culture at Coca-Cola Consolidated. I've taken you back over the past twenty years and described a transformation process that began when our eyes were opened and we realized that we needed to become an on-purpose company. We instituted some changes and, as a result, have learned a few things about our culture.

Because we believe we have an obligation to share our learnings with other companies and organizations, we took an even greater step of courage and developed a way to share our insights with a broader audience. We've bundled up all these lessons into a conference we call t-factor, which stands for transformation factor. These conferences serve as the platform we use to share the principles that contributed to our own culture transformation. t-factor embodies how we at Coca-Cola Consolidated are doing our best to lead courageously.

t-factor Leadership Events

The t-factor gatherings provide an experience that brings together and activates corporate and community leaders to build purpose-driven cultures, develop people who seek God, connect with their purpose, and serve and care for each other. Through in-person and virtual events, online resources, and networking opportunities, t-factor participants are equipped, empowered, and inspired to implement a purpose-driven corporate culture. These are also wonderful opportunities for us to deepen our relationships with our customers, suppliers, brand companies, and community leaders.

Transformation is the act of changing the character or condition of something within. Our t-factor leadership events are designed to help participants impact their workplace by transforming their culture. Transformation begins with committed leaders deciding, and then acting upon that decision, to create a culture that is purpose-driven, faith-friendly, and servant oriented. If you would like to create a workplace with eternal significance, it starts with your commitment to serving others and establishing a purpose-driven environment.

The next step is to operationalize your purpose by transforming into an organizational culture that honors God by serving others. Your transformed culture will yield greater benefits to each teammate, their customers, communities served, and the organization. We designed our t-factor leadership events to provide participants with a blueprint for success, making transformation a reality.

What Happens at the Conference?

These events are half conference and half summit meetings. It's like a conference because keynote speakers share insights on a variety of topics related to what we've learned about transformation at Coca-Cola Consolidated. But it's like a summit meeting because we encourage collaboration and the sharing of ideas with everyone in attendance. We desire to see everyone involved get fired up about transformation, and that comes from Q and A sessions and talks around the dinner table after the gathering.

We offer the conference in two formats. They run for either one whole day, or we spread the content out across two half-day sessions. I like the two half-day sessions because it really allows everyone gathered to soak in all the stories, ask questions, and even collaborate with one another on ideas they might have related to the content.

We begin the conference by talking about the concept of purpose, the "Why are you here?" question. As I mentioned, we believe the Bible teaches the concept of purpose. One of the key verses we like to use that touches on the concept of purpose is found in Jeremiah 29:11, NIV. It says, "'For I know the plans I have for you,' declares the Lord, 'plans to prosper you and not to harm you, plans to give you hope and a future.'" The teaching at our t-factor conference centers around the concept that God has a plan and purpose for your life. You'll find the principles in this book at t-factor gatherings, live and in living color, and with the added blessing of collaborating with other people seeking the same things for their businesses and personal lives.

We believe that if you can get the purpose thing figured out, it will help you understand your priorities in your life, which will help you schedule your life. When you are supposed to be three places at the same time, what do you do? What are your priorities? What are you called to do? What are you good at? What are your gifts, passions, capabilities? These questions relate to purpose, the linchpin of transformation. A great by-product of digging into the idea of purpose is that as you begin to process and figure out your purpose, it will help you in scheduling your life. Who doesn't need that?

We Need to Talk More About Purpose

Let me share a little story with you that I believe illustrates just how important it is to talk more about our purpose with our employees.

Once we had three of the top consulting groups in the world coming in to talk to us about a big project at Coca-Cola Consolidated. The consultants were from well-known firms with stellar reputations, and our excitement was high.

The first group to come into our meeting began telling me all about their firm and their qualifications. I interrupted and said, "Hey, could we get to know each other a bit before we begin? I'd like to ask you a couple of questions."

"Sure," they said. "Fire away."

"What's your purpose in life," I replied.

Now keep in mind, these are some of the smartest people around—Harvard, Yale, MIT graduates. They always have an answer for everything. Not one of them had a clue as to what their purpose in life was. The two other groups came through, and I asked them as well. They, too, had no idea what their purpose in life was.

Understanding our purpose is vital to personal development and cultivating a company culture. But we don't talk about it enough, and we certainly don't take the time to formulate an answer to the question, "What's your purpose?"

As we learned more about our personal and corporate purpose, one of our big epiphanies was that if an individual can express a God-given purpose, then maybe our sixteen thousand teammates and their families can express a common corporate purpose. Imagine a whole company working to the tune of their God-given purpose. Now imagine those people also locked into your company's purpose, heart and soul. That's powerful stuff. Imagine the transformative impact that company can have on a local community, a state, even the country! As a leader in your company, having a mission is fine. It's what you do every day. But the power, the inspiration, and the motivation comes from the purpose.

Partnering for Transformation

As followers of Christ, I believe we are called to balance our devotion to God and our role as corporate leaders. t-factor was born out of the courageous desire the leaders at Coca-Cola Consolidated had to share their approach to building a God-honoring, purpose-driven corporate culture. Our goal is to partner with other companies whose leaders have a desire to build a purpose-driven corporate culture. These partnerships allow for a collective movement of companies with a mutual understanding and commitment to multiply their influence by faithfully stewarding the resources entrusted to them.

CHAPTER 8

· · · · · · · · · · · · · · · · · ·

AWAKENED TO TRANSFORMATION

*The same Jesus Who turned water into wine can
transform your home, your life, your family, and your
future. He is still in the miracle-working business, and
His business is the business of transformation.*

—Adrian Rogers

I often think back on the moment James and I shared in the
kitchen when I washed his feet. I've learned that often wise
leaders must quiet themselves and be intuitive and discerning as they read and respond to what is going on around them.

While I still cannot explain it, this was true in the kitchen that evening with Jan and our son, James. I was prompted by a deep desire stirring within me to convey the tender love and deep humility I felt at the responsibility and privilege of being James's father.

In his mind, he was a twenty-seven-year-old young man leaving home again, to reconcile conflicts and callings, and longing to prove to himself and others he had "figured it out." He had stepped out boldly and poured himself into his work in Africa. His previous track record of personal failures was all too familiar, and this was his opportunity to get things turned around.

With all my heart I wanted him to know I was with him, for him, and believed in him, and washing his feet was the way I was prompted to demonstrate devotion to him. It was one of the most intimate moments of our lives as father and son. I had no idea it would be the last time I would serve my son while he was alive.

THE CALL

Sitting down to lunch on a busy Tuesday afternoon, I was interrupted by a call from a number I recognized as having a Kenya country code.

"Hello, this is Frank Harrison," I said.

"Mr. Harrison, are you in a place where you can sit down?" the official said.

"Yes," I replied.

"If you can sit down, Mr. Harrison, then I suggest doing so."

It was immediately clear this was not a call bringing good

news. Fear and dread seeped through me as I found the place to sit. It's the call every parent prays they will not receive. Ours came on October 5, 2010. Reading from his passport, the woman on the other end of the line was sorry to inform me James Franklin Harrison IV was dead. That was all the information she could provide at that time.

Leadership rises in crisis. Nothing learned in school and no experiences in business prepare you for moments like this. My equipping, however, was supernatural. It came from the overwhelming presence of God and the truth of his Word leading and guiding me. My first responsibility was to go home and tell his mother this crushing news. It was my place to lead our family through devastating loss and sorrow. Almost ten years later, it is a role I still carry out. Leading is for a lifetime, regardless of what the lifetime looks like.

God provided many people to assist in the very difficult process of getting James's body and bringing him home. A portion of the long international flight to Nairobi was generously provided by a dear friend and business associate. During this difficult time, my friend graciously arranged private transportation for me to ease travel complications and facilitate my privacy and comfort. It was a tremendous blessing to have the time and space to try to process and prepare for all the necessary decisions to be made on arrival. I have flown into Nairobi numerous times, but this time I faced the hardest thing I have ever done in my life.

Upon arrival, three Kenyan women who worked for Coca-Cola, Kenya, met me. Their role was to provide important information and help facilitate the processes necessary to care for bringing James home. I soon found they were there in a much deeper and more important role than colleagues. They were there to minister to the brokenhearted and to bless our family in very personal and practical ways. Norah, a leader with The Coca-Cola Company, informed me that Kendi, another servant leader, remained with James's body throughout the night after he died. She wanted to ensure his body would not be unattended at any time. Our precious friends and second parents to James, Pastor Simon and his wife, Agnes, traveled through the night from Namanga, Kenya, to get to James's side.

As I went to identify his body, I knew he had been lovingly watched over and cared for by God's tender loving hand through these people. It was a strangely comforting sight, to see him. The words of our Sudanese friend Gabriel came back to me: "I've never seen anyone else love our people like James. He is not like any American I have ever known. He lives with us in our huts and eats our food and identifies with my people." Jan and I knew James was bold and brave and careless and reckless at times. The conditions in Africa took a toll on him and severely impacted his health, including a serious bout with malaria. Never one to complain or be attentive to his own self-care, James's work and living conditions overwhelmed his immune system, and it became totally depleted. Serious fatigue and a cough were the only things we detected the last time we spoke with him. Now we know there was so much more. I was informed by the coroner that James died alone in his sleep of acute pneumonia. Although his lifeless body was well cared for, it was clear to me he was not there. "To be absent from the body is to be present with the Lord" (2 Corinthians 5:9, KJV).

Around a year later, my wife, Jan, met Kendi for the first time in Nairobi. It was a tender and emotional time for her as James's mother; she wanted to personally thank these selfless women for all they had done. Kendi's response to her thanks was simply "Ma'am, it was my reasonable act of service." That sounds a lot like servant leadership to me!

Many others stood with us during these dark and difficult days. While I was in Africa, Jan was at home in Charlotte. She waited to receive James's three sisters from various places and began to plan and prepare for his service. Our pastor and his wife, our friends, and our family all came alongside to help carry the burden of sorrow and grief. These were extenuating circumstances, and there was an overwhelming measure of God's amazing grace and goodness poured over our family for this time.

Life without James was never on my radar. Washing his feet became so much more than a memory or a teaching moment. It is a picture of what it means for me to humbly serve and sacrificially give. To pour yourself out for the people you share life with is a gift, an honor. On the night Jesus washed the feet of his disciples, they had no idea what it meant. As the days of their lives and the reach of their ministry expanded, history proves their perpetual example of humility and serving built the church of Jesus Christ. True to his character, it is my personal experience that humility and service continue to build up people and build out the kingdom of God in our personal and professional lives.

Humility and service require fearless courage. You will risk being viewed as weak and powerless. Based on the Word of God and my own personal experiences, it is a risk worth taking.

I never expected my life without James. How quickly our best-laid plans and dreams disappear.

A LIFE LIVED ON PURPOSE

James was a courageous leader. I mentioned earlier how James wasn't afraid of anything. The fact that he accepted the challenge to jump in to make a difference in the war-torn country of Sudan in the middle of their forty-year civil war was normal fare for us. I remember years back we kept an old grumpy bison on our farm. That bison ended up killing one of our horses and would even chase people. Crazy ole bison. One day James and I were driving the truck near the pasture where we kept the bison.

"Dad, stop the truck," James said.

So, I did.

"What are you doin'?" I said as I watched James jump out of the truck, hop the fence, and walk straight toward that old crazy bison. "James, that thing's going to mess you up—get out of there."

But he paid no mind to me and kept walking. Then he started shouting, "Hey, bison! Hey, bison!" James wanted the bison to know that while other visitors to the farm demonstrated fear of it, he had no fear of it. He wanted that bison to know who was the boss. The bison just looked at James in amusement, knowing if he wanted to, he could stomp James into the ground, but after some time, James turned, proclaimed victory, and slowly walked back to the truck.

I wasn't smiling at the time. Well, maybe I was just a little. But I sure smile at that memory now. James was fearless, and nobody who knew him was surprised when he would push the limits. Others may fear the unknowns associated with Africa, but James did not.

Most of all, James enjoyed helping people. He'd befriend homeless men. He could recognize pain in people. And when he did, he didn't overlook it or discount it. It resonated in him. So when he left for Lui, Sudan, which was still embroiled in their civil war with the north, I said to myself, *Of course he'd take up this challenge.*

His experiences in Africa changed him, taking what was the very best of him and molding him into an extraordinary leader. I watched James's life transform before my eyes. But here's what's fantastic about observing someone, especially someone you love deeply, experience a wake-up call and change their life: The transformation you see in them, you end up desiring for yourself. And that was true of my relationship with my son. He wasn't content to let things stay the same. And that passion was infectious and remains his legacy.

Two years after we launched Open Eyes, I received that fateful call. But even though the personal loss was and continues to be a weight my family must bear, it also has given us all a renewed sense of passion and purpose for our efforts with our nonprofit organization and, indeed, our own personal lives. It's hard to say it, but it's true: Something beautiful came from tragedy. From loss came renewal. From wandering came purpose. From the seeking heart came transformation.

To me, James's life is a snapshot of what a life lived on purpose can look like. If you know your purpose, then transformation isn't far behind.

In discussing this final chapter, Jan and I talked—as we have so many times—about the impact and legacy James had on so many people. I want you to hear her reflections about our son and his legacy.

Reflections About James by His Mother

The years, almost ten now since James's sudden death, give perspective that real time doesn't yet have. Distance from the epicenter of your heartbreak allows the opportunity to sift and sort through the rubble of memories. Every part and piece you find are valuable in helping to better understand and appreciate the irreplaceable treasure of the son you have lost.

What is it about parents that makes them both the head cheerleader and most demanding taskmaster to a child? Is it because the minute you hold your baby you sense you are responsible for someone of inestimable worth? Every single day you search out the promise and potential within. Every single day you seek to mine character gems and detect flaws that threaten. The deepest desire of our heart is to help them become the fine-quality and highly valuable person we know they were created to be.

In hindsight, I know there were many times we hit the mark and many times we missed it with James. Why even share this? Maybe in hopes of encouraging someone who is working diligently today as a parent that shaping and refining is a very delicate set of skills. They require just the right amount of heat and pressure, and the ultimate result is a lifetime in the making. Regardless of who you are, the call to parent is more than you are qualified for. *The potential and purpose of your child is settled in the Father's heart, and it is his hand that invites you to participate with him in the gift of influencing a life.* Frank and I joined with the Creator and giver of life to raise James to know and love Jesus above all else. His young heart was tender, and he received seeds of truth and faith readily.

Early in his life we detected that compassion and kindness were an integral part of his character composition. As Frank has previously shared, James could not look away from homeless people huddled in cardboard boxes for shelter or rummaging through a garbage can for food. He not only noticed what most his age did not see but also responded with some action, great or small. He always carved out a place in his heart for the overlooked, underserved people he encountered. So, like Frank, I was not surprised when he called from the ravaged villages in Sudan and said, "Dad, we have to help these people."

As a young man trying to find himself, he found the deepest sense of purpose with people whose basic needs were overwhelming. In them he recognized something money, education, career path, and comfort could never buy. The joy he witnessed in many of the people did not rest on their circumstances. And the faith lived out in their daily survival spoke more than twenty years of polished Sunday school lessons.

James spent the last five years of his life caught in the

continued

tension of who he thought he should be and who God was calling him to be. As parents with twenty-twenty hindsight, we can see where we missed some clues. It's not always an easy path for us to discern. James's heart was planted in East Africa with the pastors and mentors he had grown to love and respect. His head was trying to figure out what that life would look like in the world he came from. Would he give up more than he would gain? Would he be abandoning a place where heritage and influence ran deep? He was neither ready nor prepared to step into business life, and the incongruousness of it all was conflicting and painful.

Many might have been surprised to hear that James started a ministry. Anyone who really knew him was not. James could be more controversial than conventional. He had tremendous vision and his own version of how to make things happen. He was a risk-taker who was not afraid to live on the edge of reckless and was not unwilling to try before he thought things through sometimes. He was a blessing and a challenge. James was, and still is, one of God's greatest refining tools in our lives.

No matter how familiar you are with the characters of Scripture, they have a greater depth of meaning when you recognize God's hand is writing your story in a personal, powerful, and often painful way. While the world—and even parents—is scrutinizing credentials, experience, and qualifying accomplishments, God's wisdom is scanning for a heart that is loyal to him.

James Harrison's heart for God was loyal. Far from perfect, there was an undying desire to get close to Jesus. Challenges and disappointments forged an unbroken conviction in the unfailing goodness of God.

The last time we spoke by phone, a few days before James's death, we prayed together. He was quick to express humble thanks to God for his goodness and faithfulness to him.

James's place in our hearts will never be empty. Love and memories combined with time and perspective continue to fill us with insights, understanding, and wisdom we are grateful for. The grace of God is sufficient for whatever he chooses to do in your life. We will spend our lifetime unearthing the unique gifts that made James who he was. There will continue to be discoveries of things we did not recognize. But in those moments, we have comfort and assurance that nothing was overlooked or misunderstood by his heavenly Father. He used James's life in ways we could have never imagined.

Just this week I listened to someone pray for a heart filled with the courage and compassion of James Harrison to be eager to go to hard and hopeless places and share life and love with people. To extend to others what we all long to have extended to ourself: "You are seen, you are valued, and you matter to me and to Jesus."

I will be a lifelong learner from James. He continues to teach me far more than I ever taught him, and that is the grace given for partnering with such a gracious and generous God.

WAKE UP, OH SLEEPER

Back in chapter two, I said something we all know, but sometimes we live as if we've forgotten its truth: Life is short. If we spend life spinning our wheels, just going through the motions, we'll miss out on everything that God has planned for us. Sometimes, like my son, James, you've got to step up and seize the opportunity when it comes your way.

But sometimes, the opportunity doesn't come your way. Sometimes you've just got to get out there and go searching; you've got to get in the mix of life and see what God is doing so that you can find your part in it. The point is, you can't sit back and watch life pass you by.

At the outset of this book, I mentioned how much I love this particular verse from the Bible: "Wake up, sleeper, rise from the dead, and Christ will shine in you" (Ephesians 5:14, NIV). Let's go a little deeper into it as we round out our discussion about all things relating to leadership.

I mentioned these questions earlier: Am I living life asleep, or am I living my life on purpose? Am I settling for the status quo, just going through the motions at work and with my family, or is there a deeper meaning behind it all? There is more I'd like you to consider.

There's something else in that verse from Ephesians. Come to find out, that verse was a hymn sung by the Christians in the early church. And why did they sing that particular verse? Because of the overwhelming transformational power of the Divine light. The ultimate transformation in life is being dead and then coming to life. Wouldn't you agree?

Other translations of that same verse say, "And *Christ will* give you light." The slight difference is amazing, because it's not suggesting that Jesus will *give* you some kind of beam of light. Instead, it means that *Jesus himself is the light* that will shine on you and make you alive.

What I love so much about the Christian faith is that it is the ultimate example of what transformation looks like. When God shines his light on you, it transforms you. Though you were dead, it says in the New Testament, yet shall you live. And when you're transformed from death to life, you actually become that light too. Why? Because the light from God that gives you light—and turns you into light—radiates through your entire being, so much so that your actions reflect the goodness and excellencies of God.

Think back with me to that list of five transformational leader attributes. The final characteristic on that list states that transformational leaders foster a life-giving culture in their home, families, and workplaces. They believe excellence honors God, and they pursue it in their personal and professional lives. They cultivate the conditions in which others can flourish and grow.

There's a lot packed into those three sentences. But I want to draw your attention to the *life-giving* nature of the transformational leader. As we've just discussed, transformation, seen in Scripture and through the eyes of God, literally takes a person from death to life. And not just any life, but abundant life, a most excellent life. Life that comes from God carries with it the power to turn the drab into a thing of excellence and beauty.

Martin Luther King Jr. said it well. In a speech he delivered to a group of students at Barratt Junior High School in

Philadelphia, six months before his assassination in 1968, Dr. King spoke of the importance of having a blueprint for life. One of the elements of your life's blueprint, he said, was excellence:

> "If it falls your lot to be a street sweeper, sweep
> streets like Michelangelo painted pictures,
> sweep streets like Beethoven composed music,
> sweep streets like Leontyne Price sings before
> the Metropolitan Opera. Sweep streets like
> Shakespeare wrote poetry. Sweep streets so
> well that all the hosts of heaven and earth will
> have to pause and say: Here lived a great street
> sweeper who swept his job well."[8]

Dr. King reminded the students that everything they do should be done as if "God Almighty called you at this particular moment in history to do it." For the person who knows and pursues a relationship with God, a transformed life shines with a kind of excellence that grows more and more rare in our world. Pursuing your best in everything not only invigorates your own work but also infuses those around you with an air of "Yeah, let's do this thing, and let's do it well." Like James's life and passion, the life-givingness of excellence—say, in vision—is contagious.

A life-giving culture in your home, family, and work through excellence looks like doing your very best in your work, but it also means striving for excellence in character as well. Excellence of character looks like contributing to the needs in your community, being the best father or mother you can be, or serving your coworkers through the thoroughness of your work. You can be the best of who you are right where you are. Dr. King finished his speech by saying:

> "If you can't be a pine at the top of the hill, be
> a shrub in the valley. Be the best little shrub
> on the side of the hill. Be a bush if you can't
> be a tree. If you can't be a highway, just be a
> trail. If you can't be a sun, be a star. For it
> isn't by size that you win or fail. *Be the*
> *best of whatever you are."*

This is what James did so well. He wasn't like anyone else, and that's exactly who God wanted him to be. And the same goes for you and me. God put us all here on this earth to do something great, and he smiles down on us when we do it so that he can see us doing our best for him—our Father who loves us for the person he knows we are.

ONE-ON-ONE

I began this book reflecting on James's legacy. I saw in my son a transformation that lives in my mind and spirit every single day. The way he led and loved was infectious, and it will forever be his legacy. That legacy continues today in Africa, India, and across the world through the nonprofit organization we started together, Open Eyes.

I really got into the word "legacy" after James died. I'd really never thought much about it before. It's a powerful concept. As we discussed earlier, it's not like inheritance, where you leave money and resources, assets and land to people.

Rather, legacy is about what you leave *in* people that goes on and on. Legacy is what people say about you after you're gone. Which, of course, makes a *real* legacy an eternal one. The only way I've been able to figure that one out is through a relationship with Christ and his promise of eternal life.

So, regardless of your age, I have a few final questions for you, my friend: How do you plan to finish life? Your career? How do you plan to finish?

Will you finish strong or just take it easy hanging out at the beach or at the mountain house? Are you going to come around third base all rested up and ease into home? Or will you round third base full speed ahead, beat up, banged up, diving right into home plate and safely into heaven. I want to be that second runner. How about you?

In Luke 12:16–21 (NIV), Jesus tells the parable of the rich fool. When the rich man had an abundant harvest, he thought he'd just build bigger barns. And then he'd say to himself, "You have plenty of grain stored up for many years. Take life easy; eat, drink, and be merry." But God said to him, "Fool! This night your soul will be demanded of you; then who will get what you have prepared for yourself?" Jesus said, "This is how it will be for whoever stores up things for themselves but is not rich toward God."

Don't waste your life. Don't withdraw. Stay in the game. The Bible implores us not to grow weary in well-doing, so I want to encourage you, regardless of the circumstances, to continue to fight the good fight and press on! The Great Commission is alive and well. It doesn't say that when you make a lot of money and move to the retirement home in the mountains that you don't have to worry about the Great Commission anymore. No! God wants us to finish life *strong* for him.

And now for you younger folks who may be resisting these questions. It's never too early to consider your legacy. I know it's easy to think, "What is all this about finishing strong? That's years away. I mean, I will get serious about the God thing down the road, when I'm in a better position, a stronger position, and have more influence. I'm not even married yet, but I'll get all that stuff done down the road."

No, no you won't. I believe if you don't get serious now, you won't do it later. You need to move now. You need to take a stand for Christ now. I recommitted my life to Christ at the age of twenty-eight. I had an awakening and said it was time to get dead serious about my walk with God. You've got to do that; you *can* do that! I want you to have an awakening because God has much ahead for you. I want you to pursue the person God made you to be.

Think for a moment on this verse. John 9:4 (NIV) says, "Night is coming, when no man can work."

The day will be gone for you at some point. Your time to have a powerful impact for Christ is limited. We need to move *now* while our day is here! Whatever you are going to do for Jesus, you better do now.

How awesome would it be if we got serious about faith in the workplace? Imagine what God can and will do if we just take that first step toward transforming our company cultures for his glory! As we start changing the marketplace, we can change everything. Let's be agents of transformation and watch God breathe life into our companies, our communities, and our countries! Let's get to it!

WORK IT OUT

Well, this was a good sit down—you and me here, sipping our Cokes and talking leadership and transformation, a crazy bison, and a purpose-driven business. We've covered a lot. Let me leave you with this. Perhaps you or others you know in the business world may think you don't really have all that much influence, that it's not that important for you to be great leaders. Or that you don't need to take risks with your businesses or in your personal lives.

I want to strongly encourage you. The truth is, your business, your organization, and your family are all your platforms for leadership, yes, but more so for your ministry—your service to God. That was my big epiphany: I'm accountable for everything that God has entrusted to me, so what am I going to do with it? And so, I leave you with the same question: What are you going to do with all God has entrusted to you, to your family, and to your business?

ACKNOWLEDGMENTS

While I could never appropriately thank everyone who made this book possible, I would like to acknowledge the exceptional contribution of a few specific people.

Thank you to the many Coca-Cola Consolidated team-mates I've worked with through the years; your dedication and commitment to living out our purpose is remarkable. There would be no book to write without you.

Tim Willard, I truly appreciate your patience and hard work in helping me complete this book. Thank you for your willingness to help me find my voice and for getting it down on paper.

To the entire team at Greenleaf Book Group, and especially our executive editor, Jessica Choi, you've made this book better.

To my loyal friend Mark Conklin, thank you for coming alongside and tying it all together. You structured our work in a meaningful and powerful way. Thank you for the endless hours you spent on this project.

To my daughters: Morgan, Caroline, and Carter, being your father is one of the greatest blessings of my life. Your love and devotion to your families and your commitment to your faith in Christ are a great source of encouragement and joy to me. Thank you for your daily example of selfless love and service to others. You continue to teach me and show me many of life's deepest and most valuable lessons. It is a privilege to watch you become women of godly influence and an honor to share life with you. I'm thankful for and very proud of each of you.

To my sons-in-law: Jay, Josh, and Ellison, you are my sons, and I love you. I am blessed by your leadership in your family and your walk with God.

And finally, to my wife, Jan—confidante, counselor, supportive helpmate, and loving mom to our four children. I am eternally grateful for your faithful influence. You know our story better than anyone and have been essential in bringing this project to completion—thank you.

Resources

For more information
about t-factor conferences:

Email: t-factor@ccbcc.com
Online: www.t-factor.com

t-factor
Transforming Workplace Cultures

*To transform workplace cultures
around the world for good, for God, for growth.*

NOTES

1. Os Hillman, "Is This Billy Graham Prophecy About the Next Great Move of God Coming to Pass?" *Charisma News*, accessed May 11, 2020, https://www. charismanews.com/marketplace/72688-is-this-billy-graham-prophecy-about-the-next-great-move-of-god-coming-to-pass.

2. "Coca-Cola History: World of Coca-Cola," *World of Coca-Cola*, accessed May 11, 2020, https://www. worldofcoca-cola.com/about-us/coca-cola-history/.

3. Kevin W. McCarthy, *The On-Purpose Person: Making Your Life Make Sense*, Updated edition. (Winter Park, Florida: On-Purpose Publishing, 2008), 14.

4. Matthew 23:11–12, "The greatest among you will be your servant. For those who exalt themselves will be humbled, and those who humble themselves will be exalted." (NIV)

5. C. S. Lewis and Kathleen Norris, *Mere Christianity*, Revised & Enlarged edition. (San Francisco: Harper-One, 2015), 124.

6. Richard Furman, MD, FACS, and David Jeremiah, "Introduction" in *Prescription for Life: Three Simple Strategies to Live Younger Longer*, Reprint edition. (Revell, 2014).

7. Jim Collins, *Good to Great: Why Some Companies Make the Leap . . . and Others Don't.* (New York: HarperCollins, 2001)

8. The Estate of Dr. Martin Luther King, Jr., "What Is Your Life's Blueprint?" *The Seattle Times*, accessed January 4, 2021, http://special.seattletimes.com/o/special/mlk/king/blueprint.html.

INDEX

ABOUT THE AUTHOR

FRANK HARRISON III officially began his career with Coca-Cola Consolidated in 1977, but his roots in the Coca-Cola system date back to 1902, when his great-grandfather, J. B. Harrison, first introduced Coca-Cola to the Carolinas. Early in his career Frank worked in a number of entry-level positions, including running routes and operating bottling lines.

He graduated from the University of North Carolina with a Bachelor of Science degree in business administration, and in 1983 he obtained an MBA from Duke University. Beginning in 1977, Frank served in a variety of operational and leadership roles throughout the company until becoming chairman and CEO in 1996.

As the fourth-generation family leader of what has become the nation's largest Coca-Cola bottler, Frank is focused on creating a culture of servant leaders whose values and actions honor God. Coca-Cola Consolidated is a public company, and Frank is constantly focused on delivering consistent and sustained value to shareholders. At the same time, he believes that God owns it all. He sees himself as the chief steward, accountable to the owner for using the resources he has been entrusted with to make a positive difference in the lives of over sixteen thousand teammates and their communities.

In 2008, Frank and his late son, James Franklin Harrison IV, co-founded Open Eyes, a public, nonprofit ministry dedicated to equipping leaders throughout the world who serve those in need, share the message of Jesus Christ, and disciple believers. Frank has personally led multiple teams to the war-torn country of Sudan, just one of the countries where Open Eyes is currently focusing its efforts.

Frank lives in Charlotte, North Carolina, but also enjoys spending time on his farm outside of Charlotte with his wife, Jan, of forty-four years; their three married daughters and sons-in-law; and their eight grandchildren.